Rooted in Tradition
Art Quilts from the Rocky Mountain Quilt Museum

THE
DONNING COMPANY
PUBLISHERS

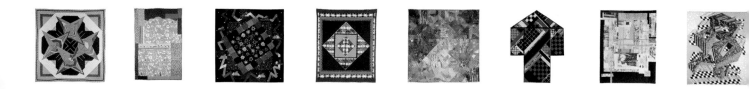

Rooted in Tradition

Art Quilts

from the
Rocky Mountain
Quilt Museum

Judith Tomlinson Trager
and Heidi Krakauer Row

Foreword by Robert Shaw

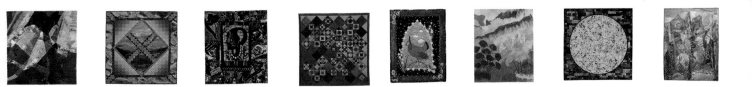

Published by The Donning Company Publishers
184 Business Park Drive, Suite 206
Virginia Beach, VA 23462

ISBN: 1–57864–314–7 (hardcover)
ISBN: 1–57864–315–5 (softcover)

Library of Congress Cataloging-in-Publication Data

Trager, Judith.
    Rooted in tradition : the art quilt from the Rocky Mountain Quilt Museum / Judith Trager and Heidi Krakauer Row ; foreword by Robert Shaw.
        p. cm.
    Includes index.
    ISBN 1-57864-314-7 (hard cover : alk. paper) – ISBN 1-57864-315-5 (soft cover : alk. paper)
    1. Art quilts–United States–History–20th century–Catalogs. 2. Art quilts–Colorado–Golden–Catalogs. 3. Rocky Mountain Quilt Museum (Golden, Colo.)–Catalogs. I. Row, Heidi Krakauer. II. Title.
    NK9112.T74 2005
    746.46'0973'07478884–dc22
                                    2005013208

Printed in the United States of America by Walsworth Publishing Company.

Acknowledgments

Many people helped to make this exhibition and catalog, trusting in my judgment and skill as a curator and writer. The warmest thanks go to the artists who contributed their rich and wonderful works to the collection and their words to the catalog. Without their commitment to the future of the art quilt and the mission of the Rocky Mountain Quilt Museum, none of this would have been possible. Equal thanks go as well to both the Board of Directors of the Rocky Mountain Quilt Museum and Nanette Simonds, their emeritus chair, for their unfailing support, and to The Art Quilt Project committee, especially Greg Katz, Theresa Petermann, Heather McHugh, Cheryl Pratt, and Pat Moore. Thanks to Martha Spark, for her tireless commitment to cataloging and managing the collection. Their efforts to get this show on the road were an inspiration. Without them, this could not have happened. Heidi Row, my collaborator and talented book designer earns my undying gratitude for her thousands of hours of work to make the book come together. Her vision about how the book should look carried me through the tedious tasks of editing, rewriting, and rethinking. Special thanks, too, to Janet Finley, retired director of the Rocky Mountain Quilt Museum, who understood the vision of growing the Museum's collection in a new way and enlisting support for that vision. And to Paula Pahl, the current Executive Director of the Museum, goes praise and gratitude. Her ability to grasp the reigns of the project mid-stream when it was moving like a juggernaut is to be commended. Thanks too, to Jenny Cook, Director of the Foothills Art Center, Golden, Colorado, for her and her staff's generous support in designing the exhibition and helping with the symposium, Rooted in Tradition: The Art Quilt. And, I will be always grateful for the support of my critique group, The Piecemakers, who question, suggest, and support my growth and development as an artist and human being. And to Trager: thank you for always being there, and especially for your cooking.

Judith Trager
Boulder, Colorado 2005

It is not often a person gets a chance to combine one's passions in life to contribute to an exciting and significant project, so I am fortunate to have had the opportunity to do so here. Thank you to Janet Finley for bringing me onboard early in the project and to Judith Trager for our exchange of ideas throughout the process. Thanks to my friend, Jeff M'lady, who took time from his busy schedule to proof the book before it went to print. A big thank you to my family who endured my many hours at the Museum and at my computer while I worked on this book and the art quilt symposium. And special thanks to my young son, Ben, who rode along with me on my many extra trips to the Museum to complete my work.

Heidi Krakauer Row
Arvada, Colorado 2005

Table of Contents

From its opening in 1990 until quite recently, The Rocky Mountain Quilt Museum focused its efforts on documenting the history of quiltmaking in its own region—the states along the Front Range of the Rockies. But after successfully building a fine collection of historic pioneer and Great Plains quilts, the museum felt it needed a new direction. It found that direction when it bravely decided to move beyond the safety of tradition and explore what the quilt of the future would be.

The museum was encouraged to embark on this somewhat risky new path in part because the Front Range region has emerged as a hotbed of studio quiltmaking activity in recent years. The Front Range Contemporary Quilters group has been the driving force in fostering and shaping this explosion of creative energy. The group's vibrant education program has exposed a generation of young artists to the possibilities of the quilt medium, and experienced teachers and artists like Faye Anderson, Patty Hawkins, and Debra Lunn have helped to lead the way.

Over the past several years, the museum's groundbreaking Art Quilt Project has dramatically redefined the institution's mission and made significant strides toward its ambitious new goal of building a comprehensive collection of quilts that would represent the history of studio quiltmaking in the United States. The museum's ultimate objective is to gather representative work by all the major artists who have been trend setters in the field of studio quilts, and to show the wide range of materials, subject matter, and technical approaches that these innovative artists have brought to the quilt medium.

This exhibition showcases the museum's growing collection of studio quilts, which at the time of this writing included works by fifty-seven artists made between the early 1980s and the present. The collection includes quilts by such historically important artists as Radka Donnell, Nancy Erickson, Jean Ray Laury, M. Joan Lintault, Terrie Hancock Mangat, Therese May, Yvonne Porcella, Joan Schulze, and the husband and wife team of Gayle Fraas and Duncan Slade, all of whom have played major roles in the evolution and advancement of studio quiltmaking. In addition to seeking the work of recognized masters and important regional artists, the museum also is betting on the work of younger artists like Laura Cater Woods and Lisa Call, who it feels have the potential to define the future of the studio quilt.

What is now called "The Art Quilt" had its beginnings in the profound social changes of the 1960s. As the counterculture flourished in the late 1960s and 1970s, a great revival of interest in quilts and other handcrafts spread across the country. Thousands of women took up quiltmaking, and collectors sought prime examples of newly discovered Amish quilts. The Whitney Museum of Art presented graphically powerful traditional quilts as prime examples of abstract design, elevating them to walls formerly reserved for paintings, prints, photographs, and other accepted visual art forms. Feminist historians reexamined women's work and pointed out the importance of quilts as artistic and historic documents that revealed the stories of American women as no other artifacts could. Pop artists like Claus Oldenberg and Andy Warhol broke down long-standing prejudices about cloth as a medium, and feminist artists such as Faith Ringgold and Miriam Shapiro challenged the academy in part by focusing attention on quilts and other traditional handwork in their art. Ringgold framed her canvases in patchwork while Shapiro worked bits of embroidery and other found textile work into her paintings, and their art and lectures profoundly influenced many younger women.

Drawn to quiltmaking by all of these forces, a growing number of young academically trained artists recognized that quilts could be art and took up the quilt as their medium of choice. Most of them were women who studied studio arts such as ceramics, painting, printmaking, and weaving before they began making quilts. All of them shared a love of working with cloth, which brought them into solidarity with the unrecognized women artists who made the great quilts they admired. But unlike those unconscious artists, they brought the design skills, techniques and compositional approaches learned in formal disciplines to the traditional and often conservative medium and changed it forever. And whereas traditional quiltmakers intended their work to be seen on the horizontal plane of a bed, they deliberately moved quilts to the gallery wall, demanding that women's art be looked at in an entirely new way.

Step by step, the early quilt artists moved away from the traditional patterns and techniques that had initially attracted them to quiltmaking, and shared their experiments and discoveries with each other. Some manipulated fabric the way an abstract expressionist painter would his oils, juxtaposing colors and patterns that shocked traditional quiltmakers. Others experimented with shapes, moving beyond the traditional square or rectangular quilt format to circles and asymmetrical forms. Some worked solely with fabric and thread, while others employed a mix of materials, including hand-dyed or printed cloth, paint, fiber reactive dyes, paper, photo transfers, metallic threads, buttons, beads, and more.

Spurred by the enormous ambition of its leading practitioners, the new movement reached a plateau of technical mastery and innovative design in the 1980s. By the early years of that decade, a critical mass of artists had been working long enough in the medium to have developed distinct and highly personal approaches to quiltmaking. In 1986, seventeen of those cutting edge artists were championed in an exhibition that finally gave their unorthodox work a name—The Art Quilt, organized by Michael Kile and Penny McMorris.

Almost all of those seventeen artists are still at work today, and many others of equal talent have joined them over the past two decades. The small group of mavericks that broke with tradition in the early years of the art quilt movement has grown into a community of hundreds of women and men, all pushing the envelope of what the quilt can look like and mean. These artists create quilts that are abstract or realistic, beautiful or expressive, simple or complex, carefully planned or full of improvisatory surprises; they make quilts that tell a story, capture a scene or a mood, state an opinion, or simply please the eye and intrigue the mind. The crack in the door of the quilt that was opened in the 1960s is now gaping wide. There is no turning back, but this exhibition allows us to look with wonder at where quilt artists have been and feel great excitement about where they may take us in the years to come.

Robert Shaw
Shelburne, Vermont

An Exciting Convergence of Quilts

Eugenia Mitchell

It all began around a kitchen table in Golden. Eugenia Mitchell's dream was to have a quilt museum, but she needed help. Soon she recruited several friends including Jan and Warren Spaulding, Virginia Cusack, and Anna Shuck. Beginning in 1987, they met at Eugenia's house for several years but nothing happened. Finally, Anna Shuck said, "Let's either do it or give it up!" That was the catalyst to make a definite effort. The Dallas Quilt Guild gave them a grant of $500 and they were committed. The group rented one room in the Central Building in downtown Golden and the Rocky Mountain Quilt Museum opened on May 1, 1990. Excitement filled the air! The dream had come true!

A similar event was underway in 1989 in Longmont, Colorado. Six art quilters, many of them represented in this new collection, founded a new art quilt guild, Front Range Contemporary Quilters. Their dream was to foster the growth of the art quilt and develop a strong education program for its members. With the help of many dynamic and energetic art quilters from the area, their vision is now a reality.

The two groups, the little Museum and the dedicated group of art quilters, were on lines of convergence; all that was needed was a catalyst. That came in the form of Judith Trager, an internationally known art quilter, curator and former president of Front Range Contemporary Quilters. She suggested that the Museum and the art quilt community work together on a project that would offer both a look into the future as well as the past. That point of contact became the current exhibit of art quilts at the Rocky Mountain Quilt Museum.

Hiwan Homestead
quilt by Eugenia Mitchell, 1979, from the RMQM permanent collection.

The initial collection is still at the Museum. It includes quilts made or acquired by Eugenia over a period of twenty-five years. One of the quilts depicts the Hiwan Homestead in Evergreen. Eugenia went up there, sat on a rock and drew a picture of the building, and then designed and made a quilt. Another quilt is embellished with tatted and crocheted doilies that she acquired from thrift shops. And yet a third is made from handkerchiefs collected by Eugenia's frugal mother during the Depression as premiums for going to the movies. They were stored in the closet for many years until Eugenia made a delightful and colorful quilt of them. Each one is more than a quilt; it is a textile stitching together creativity and history.

The Museum's collection has grown since 1990 through gifts and purchases. Many people have donated quilts to help broaden the collection for the benefit of the public and to assure a safe haven for a family masterpiece. The Collections Committee evaluates the content of the collection, advises the Board of Directors on needed acquisitions and encourages donations through its many contacts.

Which brings us to the exhibit, Rooted in Tradition, represented in this catalog. Over the years the Museum and Colorado art quilters have had a shared purpose of encouraging, exhibiting and celebrating the art of quilting and many art quilters have been volunteers at the Museum. The growth of the Museum's collection needed to include art quilts.

To that end, we sought quilts from important artists all over the world. To our gratification, more than fifty artists donated one or more quilts to the Museum's permanent collection, making it one of the most preeminent repositories of contemporary art quilts in the nation. This is part of a joint legacy to generations of future students and viewers. The Museum is deeply grateful for these generous gifts. The collaboration has grown out of the foresight of curator Judith Trager and the Museum's Board, and the Museum is especially grateful to two of our Collection Committee Chairpersons, Mary Ann Schmidt and Martha Spark. Their establishment of a collections policy and its timely review in conjunction with their knowledge of the textile art world has made this connection possible.

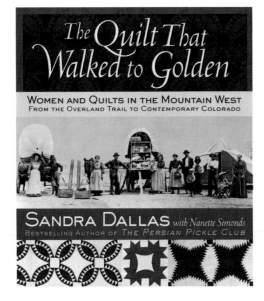

The Museum's goal is to seek and acquire quilts representative of special eras in American quilt history as well as those by notable quilters, both past and present. The Museum desires to have one of the finest collections available for education, exhibition, research, historians and visitors. A further goal is to be truly representative of the quilt history and culture of our western region and acknowledge the contributions of those who came to or passed through the American West.

A vigorous museum does more than present exhibitions. The Rocky Mountain Quilt Museum also provides strong educational programs for youth as well as adults. Our education program includes a program for young Girl Scouts who are guided through the requirements for several storage issues to the history of quilts during various eras such as the Civil War, the Colonial Revival and the Depression. We have a traveling education program that takes quilts to area schools. Quilt research and documentation procedures are also taught. As a result of this comprehensive program, visitors and members come from across Colorado, the nation and many foreign countries to be part of The Rocky Mountain Quilt Museum.

A major step in 2004 was the launch of our new publication program with the book, *The Quilt That Walked to Golden*, that tells the story of the Museum and its founder, Eugenia Mitchell, as well as regional quilt history from 1869 to 2000. The Museum is grateful to Sandra Dallas, award-winning author and former Board member, for her leadership in this project; to Povy Kendal Atchison for her photography; and to Cindy Harp for her quilt pattern adaptations.

The fifteen years of our history have been exciting and compelling. The Museum's plans for the future are equally so. In 2005, its fifteenth anniversary, the Museum will present several outstanding exhibits, including this landmark exhibit of art quilts, and will host the twenty-fifth anniversary conference of the American Quilt Study Group, an international quilt research organization. Long-term plans call for expansion of our collection, programs and facilities for welcoming, educating and serving the public. In short, the Rocky Mountain Quilt Museum is on the march and enjoying the trip.

Whether you are viewing the exhibit at the Museum or seeing it as it travels the country, we invite you to savor its beauty, its creativity, and its historical significance. For us, it's another dream come true: the joyous convergence of quilt history and quilt art.

Nanette Simonds
Past President, Board of Directors
Rocky Mountain Quilt Museum

Rooted in Tradition: The Art Quilt

But underlying virtually all my designs is that enduring influence of American patchwork—
the repeated block or unit, coupled with groups of inlaid strips.
~ Alison Schwabe, Montevideo, Uruguay, 2004

Women around the world have always made quilted clothing, bed coverings, even saddle blankets and wall coverings designed to keep the cold out of their shelters in winter. When we thought of a quilt in mid-twentieth-century America, we most often thought of those beautiful, colorful, intricate, sometimes utilitarian coverings made for our beds by a much-loved female relative. These were patchwork quilts, pieced out of cast-off fabrics and scraps that had a second life as something to warm, comfort and add beauty to one's home. But there has always been another side to the quilt as well: quilts made for show—art pieces really, often elaborately pieced, specially dyed, embroidered, appliquéd, painted. Baltimore Album Quilts were such quilts—quilts made specifically for show. Another category of specialty quilts was Crazy Quilts, so called for their construction technique. These quilts triggered a trend that lasted more than fifty years. Crazy Quilts were never used for bed coverings. Instead, they graced piano tops, backs of sofas, and sometimes even hung on walls. These "fancy" quilts were made by women with leisure time and employed all the technical sewing skills handed down to them by female relatives.

The Depression and World War II changed American women's ability to make quilts requiring leisure time and expensive materials. Women were moving from the farms and into the workforce, and time for hobbies and crafts was becoming limited. From the 1930s to the 1960s, quilts in America became more utilitarian, gracing only beds. And with the invention of synthetic fabrics, it seemed quilts and quilting would be relegated to history. By the late 1950s it just wasn't fashionable—or more importantly, modern—to have a quilt on a bed anymore. We had polyester throws, fluffy comforters and something called electric blankets. Older women were certainly still making quilts, but the skills were not often passed down to the modern women out in the workforce helping to support their families.

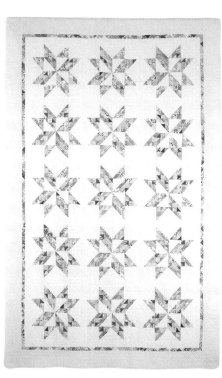

Twinkling Stars by Alice Melum Moss, Evanston, IL, ca. 1930. RMQM permanent collection.

Here and there pockets of quiltmaking remained in America, mostly among insular groups. Church quilting bees were ongoing. Quilts were still being produced in quantity in Appalachia and among the black communities in the South. Mormon girls were taught to quilt as part of their overall religious education program. Quilting flourished in the Amish and Mennonite communities in Ohio, Pennsylvania and Iowa. But in the cities and the burgeoning suburbs of both coasts, quilting was a novelty remembered by many as a treasured activity of their grandmother's era.

Quilts had not passed entirely from our consciousness, however. The explosion of color that marked the 1960s and 1970s made people begin to think about quilts again. In a late 1960s magazine story about designer Gloria Vanderbilt's home, quilts were everywhere—decorating beds and walls, used as throws, pillows and accessories. Young women were wearing long patchwork skirts. Patchwork shirts and vests for men were popular. Quilts, both old and new, were showing up at craft fairs and being featured in shop windows in trendy New York boutiques.

In 1966, Jean Ray Laury, a California fiber artist and quilter, published *Applique Stitchery*, a book that introduced many closet quiltmakers to a new way of looking at and making quilts. In the book, she emphasized simplicity, making one's own patterns and the importance of color.

Jean Ray Laury

She followed that book with *Quilts and Coverlets* in 1970, expanding on her original ideas and incorporating many non-traditional quilts made by makers, such as M. Joan Lintault, who have become pioneers in the art quilt field. The book revolutionized thinking about quiltmaking. The repeated block was still in evidence, as it is today, but elements of freedom were added. Not all the blocks were the same size in any one quilt; patterns changed within the piece; and the piece didn't have to be for the bed, it could hang on the wall. Here quilters were given permission to go beyond the block and even to make up their own patterns.

But probably the most important spark that ignited the quilt renaissance was the ground-breaking 1979 exhibition of Amish quilts at the Whitney Museum of American Art in New York, curated by Jonathan Holstein. This exhibition took a look at quiltmaking as a serious art form and exposed thousands of people to an indigenous and lively tradition. Suddenly quilts were being appreciated as art—and they were hanging from museum walls. This homely art form had found an audience and a whole new group of proponents who were soon to be practitioners and collectors.

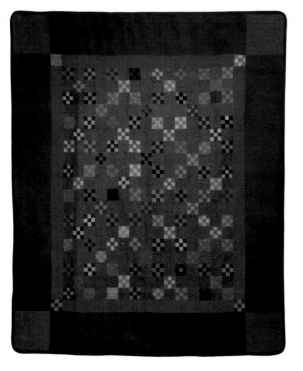

After the show, people who made quilts all over the country began to think of themselves not simply as "quilters," but "artists." Academically trained artists such as Debra Lunn, Nancy Crow and Jan Myers-Newberry were abandoning weaving to explore the freedom that came from working with commercially made cloth. Ten years later, Julie Silber and Diana Leone organized one of the most significant exhibitions on the history of the American quilt, "American Quilts: A Handmade Legacy" at the Oakland Museum. The show attracted record crowds and the accompanying film, *Quilts in Women's Lives*, by Pat Ferrero, profiled women making nontraditional quilts as art. One of those artists, Radka Donnell, then of Stanford University, had moved from painting to making quilts.

Amish Nine Patch *quilt from the collection of Pat Moore, Arvada, CO*

"I started exploring what fabrics could do to make me at home with art, with myself, with life, and I have not stopped doing that, whichever one or the other of these issues predominated. The then-and-now ongoing discussion on what *ART* is, what it is *NOT*, and *WHO* is a real artist I found off-putting and looked mostly for company and kindness."

THE BEGINNINGS

…[I]n 1975, I bought a book by Jean Ray Laury and made my first quilt, an appliquéd flag tree in red, white and blue with hand quilting, machine quilting and tying. I fell in love with quilts and took classes. This was a time of great excitement, there were few rules, little available information and every quilt was an experiment.
~Sylvia M. Einstein, Belmont, Massachusetts

In 1979, one of the most important steps in moving the quilt from the bed to the wall occurred. Nancy Crow, a fiber artist and quilt maker living in Ohio and several other artists, including Francoise Barnes, organized the first national exhibition of quilts that didn't fit the traditional mode. These quilts were colorful, freeform, wonderfully artistic and different but many of them still used the repeat block as their underlying structure. The exhibition took place at its permanent home, The Southeastern Ohio Arts Center, also called The Dairy Barn, a historic barn perched on top of a hill just beyond the city of Athens. A perfect venue for what were then called "contemporary quilts," the exhibition was designed as a showcase for quilts meant not for the bed but rather the wall. Along with the exhibition, a widely distributed catalog was published of the quilts. People began to understand quilts in a different way than before: They needn't be functional, and they needn't follow any prescribed pattern or technique. They did need to fulfill the traditional definition of a quilt in at least one way, still required of artists who enter Quilt National today:

"The work must possess the basic structural characteristics of a quilt. It must be predominantly fabric or fabric-like material and must be composed of at least two full and distinct layers— a face layer and a backing layer—that are held together by hand- or machine-made functional quilting stitches or other elements that pierce all layers and are distributed throughout the surface of the work."*

However, whether the quilt was hand-pieced, machine-sewn, painted, appliquéd or embroidered was inconsequential. Quilt National was setting a new standard, and that standard was to find the best quilts that could be considered art first, quilts second. Twenty-five years later, the artists accepted into Quilt National still set the standard for innovation and excellence.

Interweave by Michael James

Practically concurrent with the first Quilt National, in 1978 Michael James published his first book, *The Quiltmaker's Handbook* followed closely in 1981 by *The Second Quiltmaker's Handbook*. From the very beginning, these books were considered classic guides for novice quiltmakers. The bibliography of quilting resources was beginning and information was now available that taught anyone to make quilts.

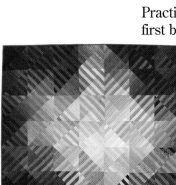

The term *art quilt* did not become standard until 1986, however, with the exhibition "The Art Quilt," curated by Penny McMorris and Michael Kiley. This traveling exhibition, which opened at the Los Angeles Municipal Art Gallery, and its gorgeous catalog, did much to bring to a wide audience the idea that quilts can be art. Many artists who had been featured in past Quilt Nationals were in this exhibition, among them Terrie Hancock Mangat, Therese May, Nancy Crow, Duncan Slade and Gayle Fraas, Erika Carter, Michael James, Yvonne Porcella and Joan Schulze. McMorris's introduction to the art quilt drew from her expertise as a quilt historian as she brilliantly tied together the history of women as makers of beautiful domestic objects and the emerging feminist artists. Patchwork was gaining in value. And recognition of art quilts by the mainstream art establishment was giving voice to those working with fiber.

* www.quiltnational.com

In 1990, Nancy Crow and Linda Fowler founded the Quilt Surface Design Symposium in Columbus, Ohio, a two-week annual school to educate artists about the art quilt. Hundreds of artists have been trained there over its fourteen years, and under the best artists in the field together as faculty, younger artists have had an opportunity to grow their artistic talents. It has attracted faculty and students from all over the world and introduced quilt makers to the study of the art quilt as not only a technical accomplishment, but also an intellectual endeavor.

THE ART QUILT TODAY

Sandra Sider, artist and quilt historian, describes the art quilt today like this:

> *Art quilts are distinguished from traditional contemporary quilts by the artists who are creating them, much like fine art photographs are distinguished from production photography. Anyone with technical expertise and serious artistic intent can create an art quilt. Whether such a quilt is good art depends on the same general criteria by which we evaluate other media, namely integrity and originality. Quilt artists create their own patterns—when indeed they use them—and often make their own fabric designs with surface design processes. The common thread connecting all quilt artists consists of the quilting itself, whether by hand or machine, with thread, staples, safety pins, dental floss, etc. Joining together the various layers creates the final structure as well as the final textured surface, with lines of quilting often "drawn" in counterpoint to other elements in the design. If art quilts can be characterized by a single word, it would be "innovation." As summarized by Hilary Morrow Fletcher, Quilt National Project Director, quilt artists "are expanding and adding to the rich vocabulary of the heritage quiltmakers and they are transforming color and texture into dynamic patterns that provide new visual experiences."* [1999 Quilt National catalog]

Gundagai by Alison Schwabe

Today, art quilts are made and exhibited by artists throughout the world. Major exhibitions in Europe, Australia, the Americas and Asia feature them. Men have joined the movement, many of them moving from other disciplines such as painting, sculpture and architecture.

Quilt exhibitions, both art and traditional, attract huge crowds to museums and galleries in the United States, and organizations such as the International Quilt Association, the Pacific International Quilt Festival and the American Quilters Society hold giant quilt conferences yearly, drawing more than a hundred thousand participants, both traditional and art quilters. Quilts and their social history are now the subject of academic research in universities like the University of Nebraska at Lincoln, where the International Quilt Study Center has

been established, and Michigan State University, which has compiled an extensive Quilt Index. Organizations such as the American Quilt Study Group and the Alliance for American Quilts are gaining support and recognition. And, with the establishment of Studio Art Quilt Associates in 1990, quilt artists have their own professional organization focusing on the business of art quilts. In addition, museums are beginning to recognize the importance of the art quilt to their permanent collections. And many of these quilts are still based on the time-honored repeated block.

Checker Cab by Mary Mashuta

THE ART QUILT PROJECT

One in Every Crowd
by Gretchen Hill

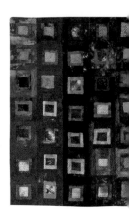

Long known as an area that is very friendly to fiber art, Colorado has a dynamic and active quilt community. Besides the many regional guilds, the Colorado Quilting Council has more than thirteen hundred members who meet regularly throughout the state to share quilt information and learn about quilts. Smaller, but just as active, Front Range Contemporary Quilters is an organization devoted to the growth, education and promotion of the art quilt. Founded in 1988 by six beginning art quilters, Diana Bunnell, Gretchen Hill, Marilyn Dillard, Patty Hawkins, Jo Fitsell Coffin, and Laura DeKloe, the organization has grown to more than three hundred members. Front Range Contemporary Quilters' education program brings the best teachers working in the quilt medium to Colorado three times a year for workshops. It has an aggressive exhibition program and has curated a traveling exhibition, "Elements from the Front Range Contemporary Quilters," which will begin exhibiting in museums in 2005.

More than fifteen members of Front Range Contemporary Quilters have been juried into Quilt Nationals, beginning in 1987. One year alone, 1995, seven Colorado artists were part of the exhibition. And at least eight members have been juried into Quilt National's parallel exhibition, Quilt Visions (held at the Oceanside Museum, California, in opposite years).

Dreams *by Faye Anderson*

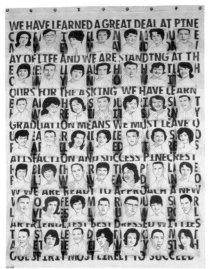

In this fiber-rich environment with powerful support organizations and extraordinary quilt artists, it was only natural that The Art Quilt Project should be established.

The Rocky Mountain Quilt Museum was founded in 1990 in Golden, Colorado, with the mission of collecting and exhibiting quilts relating to the Rocky Mountains. Started with a gift of traditional quilts collected by Eugenia Mitchell, a local Golden quilter, the museum opened in a storefront on tourist-frequented Washington Avenue. Throughout its first fifteen years, the museum actively sought to collect the best historical quilts from this region. In 2002, the then-executive director of the museum, Janet Finley, realized that in order for the museum to grow and flourish in the new century, it needed to change its mission to include not only historic and traditional quilts, but art quilts as well.

To this end, Finley asked Judith Trager, a Colorado art quilter and independent curator, to become part of the collections process of the museum. Trager, a longtime proponent and champion of the art quilt, agreed but suggested that despite the richness of talent in the area, the board of directors should look beyond the Rocky Mountain region for artists to showcase. Her proposal was simple: Collect at least sixty quality art quilts from accomplished and noted artists regardless of geography. These artists may have had Colorado connections—perhaps they once lived here or they had been here to teach. In addition, to launch this new collection a traveling exhibition should be mounted and, if possible, a catalog published.

More than seventy quilt artists were contacted and asked to donate quilts to the collection. To our immense surprise and gratification, more than fifty responded affirmatively. Several artists have donated two quilts, each from different points in their careers. Many of these artists are pioneers in the field: Yvonne Porcella, a ground-

Fran Skiles teaching a workshop at FRCQ

breaking fiber artist and the first art quilter to have her work permanently collected by the Renwick Gallery of the Smithsonian Institution; M. Joan Lintault, an innovator who has worked in the field since the 1960s and was a pioneer in using printing techniques to change the surface of her quilts; Debra Lunn and Ann Johnston, longtime Quilt National participants and the artists responsible for the hand-dyeing revolution among makers; Jean Ray Laury, author of the first significant quilt book that took quilts out of traditional pattern making and into free-form design; Terrie Hancock Mangat, who was the first to combine painting techniques with quilting techniques, using the quilt form as canvas; Caryl Bryer Fallert, who made a well-traveled path between art quilts and the traditional quilt world through her teaching and lecturing worldwide; Michael James, whose quilts bridged the gap between fine art and craft from the very beginning of the movement and who has been honored as both an NEA fellow and a fellow of the American Crafts Council; Carolyn Mazloomi, whose quilts crossed cultural, spiritual and artistic boundaries; and many others. Many of the quilts in the collection have been exhibited in Quilt National, Visions, or The Art Quilt. The collection also sought to showcase work from younger, upcoming artists, such as Laura Cater-Woods, Sandra Woock and Lisa Call.

Yvonne Porcella

All of the artists in the collection are still working artists in the quilt medium. Some have been engaged in this field for more than forty years. This exhibition and collection catalogs not only the movement, but also the growth of these individual artists and the flowering of their art.

Because the traditional mission of the Rocky Mountain Quilt Museum has been historical, The Art Quilt Project strives to chronicle the history of the art quilt, from its earliest recognition—as something separate and apart from those quilts created for the bed—to the present. Several of the quilts in the collection were made in 2004; other quilts come from the early 1980s. And, the bulk of the collection comes from the watershed decade of the 1990s. Quilts in the collection are as diverse as the makers. They are the personal expressions of very diverse artists from very diverse backgrounds and regions. Thoughtful, colorful, joyful, puzzling, even sometimes difficult, these works express viewpoints often found in the more traditional disciplines of painting, photography and sculpture. Variation in technique is the only uniformity: quilts are pieced, sewn, painted, deconstructed, collaged, some are digital images—a very twenty-first-century innovation.

Detail of
The New Holocaust
by Marta Amundson

Detail of Watermark "D"
Delta *by Gayle Fraas and*
Duncan Slade

They are appliquéd and embroidered. Some have objects sewn onto them, such as sequins and birthday candles. Quilts may be made of fabric, paper and sometimes metal. And they all declare the unique joy of creation such work gives. This collection offers the viewer a path from what was traditionally thought of as women's work to cutting edge fine art. It is not a straight path—there are no straight paths in art, like life. But it is a path that sends the viewer on an exciting journey, a journey into the past and the future of the art quilt.

Section One

Art Quilts of the 1980s:
Rooted in Tradition

Since I began quiltmaking,
I have used paint and
dye in various ways,
added beading and
other embellishments,
and no doubt will again.
But underlying virtually
all my designs is that
enduring influence of
American patchwork—
the repeated block
or unit, coupled with
groups of inlaid strips.

Alison Schwabe

Contemporary quilts came to prominence during the American Bicentennial, after being the stepchild of the arts-and-crafts movement in America. Suddenly, everyone was making quilts, and quiltmaking's visibility increased exponentially. At the Smithsonian Institution's Folk Art Festival held every summer on the Mall in Washington, D.C., in the 1980s the quilting tent was often the most popular display. Quilt festivals like the one in Kutztown, Pennsylvania, were being established. Women who had sought their traditional roots in the 1960s found an expressive voice in the quilt medium and began making quilts that varied from the repeated block. Academically trained artists like Miriam Shapiro, Robert Rauschenberg and Judy Chicago were using quilt forms in their paintings and embroideries. Women who had made clothing for themselves and their children suddenly saw sewing as something artful and creative. Quilt shops were springing up. Fabric printers were beginning to develop new lines of fabric designed especially for quilts. And some of the quilts being made were, in Robert Shaw's words, "innovative and unconventional." They were certainly contemporary. With the beginnings of Quilt National in 1979 and the Holstein exhibition of Amish quilts at the Whitney Museum in New York that same year, many quilters who had been making traditional patterns felt emboldened to call themselves artists. Although the term *art quilt* would not come into general use until 1989 with publication of the catalog from Penny McMorris and Michael Kiley's blockbuster exhibition, "The Art Quilt," it was unquestionable that the quilts being made by many artists were indeed Art.

The Celebration *by Faye Anderson*

The Rocky Mountain Quilt Museum's collection includes eight quilts from the 1980s by pioneering quilt artists. Each quilt is unique not only in subject matter but also in technical approach. From Marilyn Chaffee's *Tetrad I* that reworked a much-loved traditional eight-pointed star pattern, and Therese May's *Basket,* an early example of painting on the quilt top, to M. Joan Lintault's important quilt, *Heavenly Bodies* that used Xerox transfer on fabric, this strong group of art quilts is a harbinger of innovations that came into general use in the next decade. These eight quilts, shown in chronological order, are prime examples of the expansion of the medium. Tafi Brown's quilt, *Jewells,* is printed on muslin using photographic cyanotype chemicals. Janet Page-Kessler's quilt, *Still Life V/VI,* combines machine embroidery with traditional appliqué techniques. Yvonne Porcella's *Kimonos in My Kimono House* moved strip piecing from traditional Seminole patchwork to a new level. And Radka Donnell's *Outdoor Joys* showed how fabric could be used as an element in a color-field painting.

M. Joan Lintault
New Paltz, New York
Heavenly Bodies   77" x 77"   1980

Xerox transfers on poly/cotton, pieced, quilted.

I come from a family of storytellers. Their stories grew and grew with each telling, embroidered with embellishments and flourishes. They are the threads that bind us together, generation to generation, creating history with stories. When asked, "If you were left on a desert island what would you bring with you?" I always reply, "a good storyteller."

Everyone loves a story, comic books, manga, films, books, scrolls, folk tales, plays, gossip and rumors. A storyteller is a carrier of news, a teller of tales and the bearer of messages. Stories are the way to explain the surrounding physical world.

I am using the idea of portrait and the expressive form of visual images to tell stories. My portraits are also composed of surrogate images. Each image will contribute to the story. In my work I will give you the cast of characters. I leave it to you to make up the story.

I began making quilts in 1965 and finished my first one in 1966. I saw the bed as a large flat place to display them. Quilts are lovely things, soft, textural and inviting. I always want to make work for the palace. Nevertheless I quickly moved to the wall but still called them quilts. In the beginning I quickly lost patience with hand sewing and store-bought fabric. In 1963 I began a quest to learn all I could about dyeing and creating images on cloth. I am still learning.

I always thought of my work as art. Why would it be anything else since I did go to art school and have created all my life? I began drawing and coloring when I was five. Here I am at this age: I still love to color, draw, paint and listen to stories.

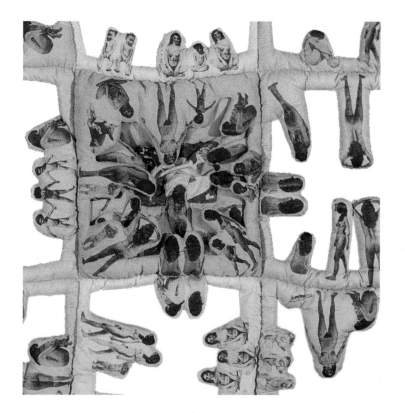

Marilyn Chaffee
Poway, California
Tetrad I   46" x 46"   1981

Commercial fabrics, machine pieced, hand quilted.

As a natural outgrowth of my early training in printmaking and applied design, my work in art quilts has been a visual journey for over twenty years. I find myself drawn to the repeated patterns and colors in my surroundings, and I am always seeking to create new and satisfying fabric constructions that reflect my personal vision.

My quilts are an extension of my lifelong love of textiles. With a BA and an MA in graphics and design, I have spent many years as an art educator. Over the years I worked with many fabric techniques including weaving, batik, appliqué and garment design. I began quiltmaking in 1980, at the beginning of the quilt renaissance that followed the Bicentennial celebration. Soon thereafter when I enrolled in a series of seminal workshops with the innovative quiltmakers of the day and became aware of the expressive possibilities of the quilt medium, I was hooked.

Tafi Brown
Alstead, New Hampshire
Jewells   62" x 72"   1982

Pieced cyanotype photographic prints on cotton using Kodalith negatives developed in dektol developer. All photographic work done by artist. Commercially printed fabrics. Machine pieced and embroidered. Cotton batting. Signed and dated on back of quilt. Hand quilted by artist.

I did a lot of photography for Benson Woodworking in the 1980s. This quilt's subject is one of the houses that was built by Benson Woodworking.

Radka Donnell
Zurich, Switzerland
Outdoor Joys   58.5" x 85"   1982

Commercial cottons, upholstery fabrics, dressmaker fabrics, machine pieced, raw edge appliqué, hand and machine quilted. Quilting by Claire Mielke.

"I have always looked for ground under my feet in a setting that was in turmoil, yet I strove for 'innovation' on a constructive basis." That statement by Radka Donnell captures her life. An artist, poet, writer, teacher and translator, Radka was born in Bulgaria and came to the United States as a young woman. She received her bachelor of arts degree from Stanford University, and her master of arts from the University of Colorado at Boulder. Acknowledged as one of the pioneers of the art quilt movement, she first encountered an American quilt in Boulder, Colorado. She still remembers its feel in her hands—soft, lightweight and puffy. As a mother at home looking for something to do in Lawrence, Kansas, she went to the public library and ended up in the crafts corner with books on quiltmaking. On walls in the corridor to the ladies room in the Lawrence Art Museum she saw "'the Real Thing': an eight-pointed star quilt! I fell in love with it and still see it before me." It inspires her still. "At that point, I had stopped painting. High Art Abstraction ruled, its content was dim or totally dismantled, and what I saw of painting left me cold. I started exploring what fabrics could do to make me at home with art, with myself, with life, and I have not stopped doing that, whichever one or the other of these issues predominated."

After making traditional patterns, Radka began to take advantage of the freedom crazy quilt designs had to offer. Seeing many of the issues in the art quilt movement and the women's movement as interrelated, her work became self-confident and expressive as she learned to speak her mind and soul. "I experienced early on the quiltmakers' struggle for cultural recognition as an issue of personal liberation—a connection no other endeavour has given me. Making quilts, studying them, talking about them, gives me daring, satisfaction and unceasing joy."

Radka has made more than 700 quilts throughout her forty-year career and has exhibited widely in America and Europe. She has written a book about quilts, *Quilts as Women's Art: a Quilt Poetics*, and has taught studio courses on quilts as women's art involving the theory and history of quilts at Westfield College, Simmons College and Wellesley College. Radka lives in Zurich, Switzerland, and works as a translator from German into English of catalogs, books and texts on art. She has written five books of poetry and several short novels.

Nancy Erickson
Missoula, Montana
*The Purple Woman, the Guardians
and the Sand*   78" x 51"   1984

Painted, machine stitched, appliquéd.

Nancy Erickson's powerful work, *The Purple Woman, the
Guardians and the Sand,* shows early on the ability of
quilts to bridge the gap between utility and fine art. "[My
pieces] are projections of the conditions in which living
beings find themselves in a future of time, or combinations
of future, present and prehistoric times," writes the artist
in her statement for the 1984 Needle Expressions exhibition
where this work won Best of Show. "Humans, in the visual
narrative, are only a part of the larger web, and more
often than not, the capybara or birds have become the
seers. The fabrics work themselves into a metaphor of
human political conditions, stutter and lurch toward a
sort of completion, carrying me along with them."

Already an established painter, Erickson early saw the
potential of melding the traditions together to make
something new.

Nancy grew up on a Montana cattle ranch and has lived
in Germany, Texas, the Midwest and New York. She has
her MFA in painting from the University of Montana in
Missoula. Her resume is extensive: she has exhibited in
numerous shows beginning in 1965, including many Quilt
Nationals as early as 1983. Her many commissions
include one for the University of North Dakota.

Yvonne Porcella
Modesto, California
Kimonos in My Kimono House   48" x 64"   1986

Commercial cottons, machine pieced, machine quilted.

Yvonne Porcella is an artist specializing in wearables and art quilts. She began in 1962 by making unique garments, wall hangings and quilts. Her first gallery exhibit was in 1972, and currently her work is featured in major exhibitions, art galleries and museums in the United States and abroad. Her work has toured in national and international shows of contemporary American quilt makers and is actively collected by individuals and corporations. The Renwick Gallery of the Smithsonian Institution, Washington, D.C., acquired her quilt *Takoage* in 1994.

Porcella's books reflect the development of her artistic interests. *Five Ethnic Patterns* was published in 1977, followed in 1978 by a second book featuring ethnic patterns, *Plus Five. Pieced Clothing* (1980) and *Pieced Clothing Variations* (1981) continued the evolution of her patterns and focus on wearable art. *A Colorful Book* (1986), an art book, uses her work to illustrate the design and color for which she is known. *Colors Changing Hue* (1994) teaches easy methods for fabric painting and includes patterns for projects. *Six Color World* (1997) continues the theme of fabric painting with a strong emphasis on color. *Yvonne Porcella: Art & Inspirations*, published in 1998, documents her work and offers insight into her art. *Magical 4 Patch & 9 Patch* was published in 2001. She has taught and lectured throughout the United States, Canada, Australia, Europe and Japan.

Porcella is founder and served for eleven years as president of the board of directors of Studio Art Quilt Associates. She is the thirtieth inductee of the Quilters Hall of Fame, Marion, Indiana, and was the fifth recipient of the Silver Star Award at the International Quilt Festival Houston, Texas.

She currently serves on the Board of Directors of The Alliance For American Quilts, Louisville, Kentucky, and is the designer of their raffle quilts. She is a member of the Advisory Board of the International Quilt Center, University of Nebraska, and is a member of art and letters in the National League of American Pen Women. Michigan State University has selected her as a Quilt Treasure for a documentation project archiving the history of American quiltmakers.

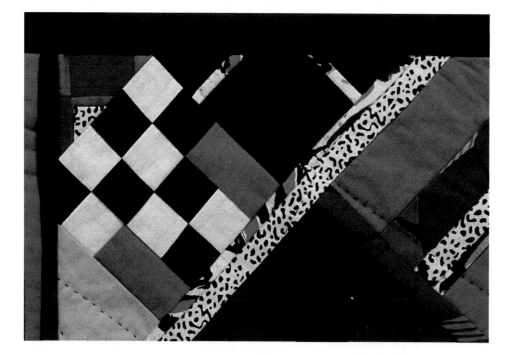

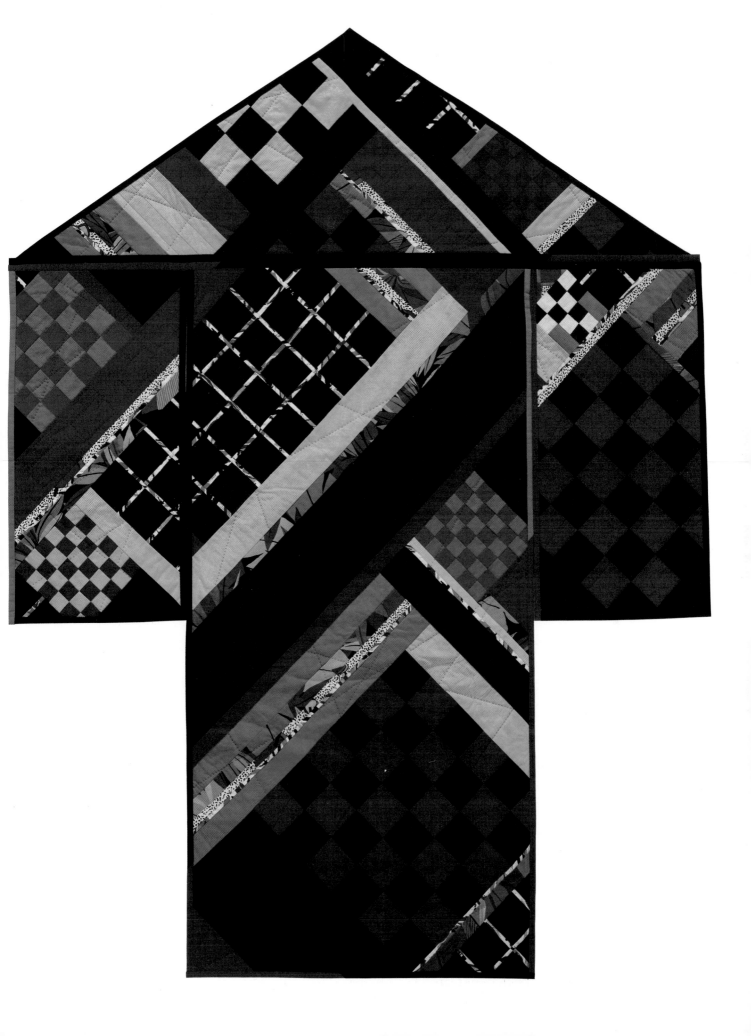

Therese May
San Jose, California
Basket   84" x 84"   1988

Commercial cottons, decorative threads, acrylics, machine pieced, machine quilted.

"In *Basket*, little white fish swim around inside the basket in the center. They've achieved something and they're protected from danger. Then there are big black monsters trying to get to the basket. They're not really dangerous, but they would like to get in because it's nicer inside. They don't really know how to get in, but they'll keep on trying until they figure it out.

"The snake is a symbol of power, and it's also trying to get inside just because it wants to give its power and love. On the very outside are big Easter eggs, and these still not only have shells around them, but they also have floating membranes surrounding them. They are still sealed inside, but these things have to be developed before they can come out."

Therese May has been a leader in the creation and development of art quilting, recognized worldwide as a guiding light in the movement and one of its most inspiring advocates. Honored as both artist and teacher, she has exhibited her work at the Smithsonian Institution in Washington and the Louvre in Paris.

Among Therese's many awards are the Most Innovative Use of Medium award in Quilt National '85 and the Quilts Japan Prize in Quilt National '95. Her work is published in numerous books and magazines, including *The Art Quilt* and *America's Glorious Quilts*. Her 1969 quilt *Therese* was selected as one of the one hundred best American quilts of the twentieth century.

Therese began making quilts in 1965 and has exhibited throughout the United States, Europe and Japan. With a focus on transformational healing, her work is centered on wholeness, integration and creativity through art and the quilt-making process. To realize and continue this focus, she makes herself available as a teacher, leading workshops for groups as well as providing individualized one-on-one sessions. She has appeared on the television show *Simply Quilts* and has taught at Arrowmont School of Arts and Crafts; the Cleveland Institute of Art; Cabrillo College; the University of California, Santa Cruz, Department of Art and Design; and the University of Minnesota Split Rock Arts Program, as well as in many quilt guilds.

In addition to Therese May's other awards and recognitions, she was commissioned twice to create quilts for the City of San Jose, and her two 196-square-foot works hang in the San Jose Convention Center. Therese has been part of the San Jose art community for the past thirty-seven years and has participated in all but two of the Silicon Valley Open Studios. She holds a bachelor of arts degree in painting and a master of arts degree in design, with emphasis on the art quilt.

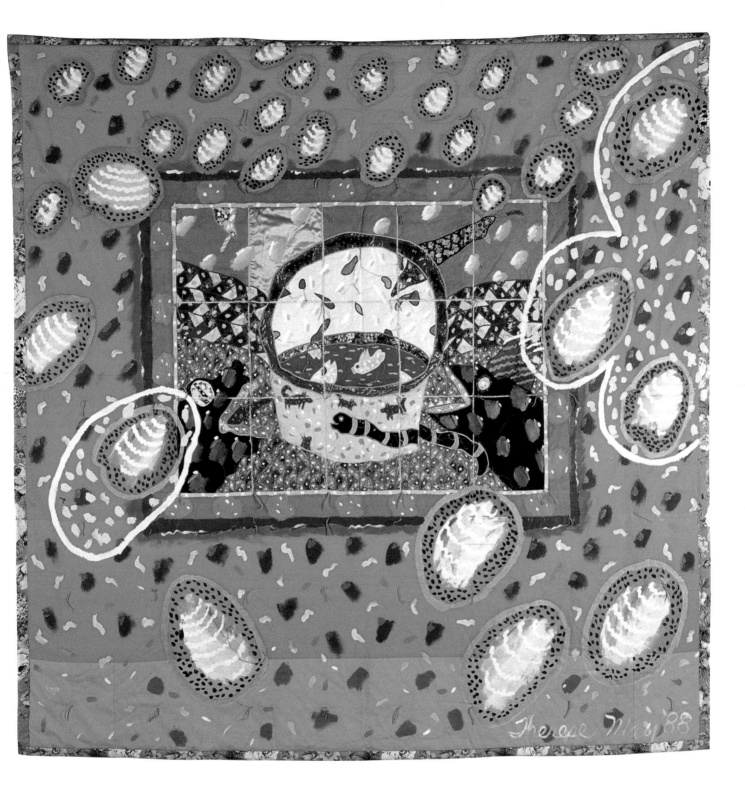

Janet Page-Kessler
New York, New York
Still Life V/VI 50" x 22"   1989

Commercial fabrics, hand painted and embroidered. Machine appliquéd, machine quilted.

"Nature was the inspiration for the Still Life series. In drawing flowers I found myself involved in a trancelike state of concentration while discovering the intricacies and beauty of the shapes and the incredible range of colors within just one bloom, colors that most of us would never imagine using together. Georgia O'Keeffe said, 'Whether the flower or the color is the focus I do not know. I do know the flower is painted large to convey to you my experience with the flower—and what is my experience of the flower if it is not the color… Maybe in terms of color I can convey to you the experience that makes the flower of significance to me at that particular time.' My own personal experience of a lily is conveyed in *Still Life V/VI*."

Born and raised in New York City and educated at the Parsons School of Design, Page-Kessler received an early introduction to quilting. Her paternal grandmother, an English immigrant, taught her English paper piecing in the late l930s. As a young mother, Page-Kessler immersed herself in

painting, photography and needlework as a way of exploring other means of artistic expression, but ultimately returned to fabrics and stitching as her preferred medium.

The Still Life series, begun in 1987, is now most representative of Page-Kessler's work. These are incredibly sophisticated compositions, using organic shapes and brilliant colors. There are often as many as fifty to sixty different fabrics in each piece, some hand-painted and embellished with embroidery. This series has received wide recognition and has been exhibited nationally and internationally. Two pieces from this series have been juried into Quilt National '89 and '91. *Still Life IX/X* was chosen from more than 800 entries to be exhibited with the Fabric Gardens exhibition at EXPO '90 in Japan and other venues in the United States.

In addition to her own work, for the many years Page-Kessler has worked with VIP/Cranston Printworks designing all of their sample quilts. She received a TOMMY award nomination for Design Excellence from the American Printed Fabrics Council in 1988. Her work has appeared in numerous publications including: *Fiberarts Design Books 3* and *4*; *Quilts in America*; *Quilts, The State of the Art*; *The New Quilt*; *Celebrating the Stitch*; *Contemporary Embroidery of North America*. She conducts workshops throughout the country and is the founder of the annual Art Quilt Network-NY, a symposium for quilt artists from around the country.

Section Two

Art Quilts of the 1990s:
The Watershed Years

Since I didn't
know the rules,
I was free to
break them
and to achieve
the kind of
spontaneity
I was seeking.

Dominie Nash

Art quilts of the 1990s marked a watershed in quiltmaking. It was a decade of incredible experimentation, energy and enthusiasm; a time filled with symposia and classes; a time when the art quilt was beginning to be taken seriously as a new medium that could compete with painting and the academic arts. Thousands of quilters were no longer calling themselves "quilters"—instead they began calling themselves fabric artists, quilt artists or just artists. A revolution was taking place in the quilt world. At festivals and fairs, there were separate categories for art quilts and innovative quilts. An art quilter, Caryl Bryer Fallert, won the grand prize at both the American Quilters Society show in Paducah and the International Quilt Association Festival in Houston.

Technique was changing, redefining, simplifying and borrowing from the traditional fields of painting and collage. Artists began to develop their own distinct and recognizable styles, leading members of quilt show juries to ask, "Is this a quilt by a famous maker?" in seeking to affirm whether a quilt was the work of a gifted student or a teacher.

Art quilters went on the road teaching, lecturing, doing trunk shows. Nancy Crow and Linda Fowler established the Quilt Surface Design Symposium, an intensive summer workshop drawing hundreds of eager students each year. And art quilts began to be recognized by major museum venues, including the Houston Museum of Fine Arts, the Columbus Museum of Art and the Folk Art Museum in New York City.

The materials quilts were made of were changing as well. Ann Johnston and Debra Lunn taught hand-dyeing to a whole generation of quilters. It was no longer necessary to depend on commercial fabric companies to have the perfect color for the ever-expanding palette. In addition to the traditional appliquéd and pieced quilts, quilts were painted (such as Nancy Erickson's *Hand Shadows*), free motion stitched, tucked and distressed. Some were appearing with photographic images that had been transferred to fabric. Arturo Alonzo Sandoval's quilts included Mylar and photographic film. Quilts even were made of screening, wood bark and

Corona 2: Solar Eclipse *by Caryl Bryer Fallert*

other nontraditional materials. Embellished quilts, such as those of Jane Burch Cochran and Betsy Cannon added to the excitement. "Anything goes" became the guiding principle of quiltmaking in the 1990s. Improvisation became the buzzword.

Thirty-two powerful art quilts from the 1990s are included in the Rocky Mountain Quilt Museum's collection. They show the progression of the medium from the dependence on the traditional block, as in Marilyn Dillard's colorful *Tallahassee Lassie II* and *III* to the painted canvas of Fran Skiles's *Thread Bare II* and back again to Sylvia Einstein's 1999 quilt, *Requiem for an Ash Tree*. These quilts expand the medium as well in ways formerly unacceptable among quilters, exploring political themes (Terrie Hancock Mangat's *Desert Storm*, Mary Mashuta's *Exploration–Learning to Get Along* and Marta Amundson's *The New Holocaust*), story telling (Jane Dunnewold's *Baby Quilt* and Sally Sellers's *Volume One*) and internal landscapes (Dominie Nash's *Peculiar Poetry 10*, Diana Bunnell's *Sewing Down the Bones* and Patty Hawkins' *Reflections #3*). Diverse, colorful, sometimes challenging, these art quilts show the medium at its height and their makers at the pinnacle of their craft. And more importantly, all the artists in the Museum's collection are still making quilts, building on the skills they mastered. This watershed decade created a path that led to the art quilts of the new century.

Faye Anderson
Broomfield, Colorado
R.E.M.　96.5" x 99.5"　1990

R.E.M.—Rapid Eye Movement emphasizes the importance of a good night's sleep in resolving design/composition challenges. Silhouettes of sleeping heads surround the quilt's border. It is made of 100 percent cotton fabric, hand-dyed by Debra Lunn and is machine pieced, hand appliquéd, and hand quilted. The quilt has been in numerous shows, most notably Quilts Now at the Zephyr Gallery in Louisville, Kentucky, in 1992 and the Oklahoma Art Museum in 1994. It won first place in the Theme category of the American Quilter's Society contest in 1991 and first place in the Colorado Artist Craftsmen annual exhibition in the same year.

Marilyn Dillard
Placitas, New Mexico
Tallahassee Lassie II and *III* 31.5" x 31.5" 1991

Commercial and hand dyed fabrics, rick-rack, machine pieced, hand quilted.

Moving to Colorado from southern California in the early 1970s was the beginning of my long-time involvement with fiber arts. At this time the words "fiber arts" were young in the arts-and-crafts environment and so was I. My Niwot, Colorado, studio was filled with yarns and three looms that were used to make handwoven rugs. I entered my rugs in juried exhibitions and was surprised to have them acknowledged with numerous awards. I taught classes locally and sometimes traveled throughout the Southwest to present guild workshops and programs. Professional publications like *Interweave Press* and *The Weaver's Journal* often featured my work.

After twenty years of weaving, I turned my attention to cloth and its role in the evolution of the American quilt. The studio that was once filled with looms and yarn was newly groomed to include sewing equipment and stacks of yardage. I was drawn to quilt making by the fabric: its color, softness and texture. Without an awareness of any traditional quilt making rules, I worked spontaneously, cutting and placing shapes onto a background. This manner of working pushed my creative senses to a new horizon. The following years my work was included in many exhibitions. Since 1990, my quilts have been exhibited in eleven states, Japan, the United Kingdom and Finland and was included in Visions: The Art Quilt, 1993, and Quilt National 1995. Private collections and a few corporate collections include works from the late 1990s.

In addition to developing my own work it has been a pleasure to participate in local fiber art groups. I was one of six women who founded the Front Range Contemporary Quilters in Colorado and served as the organization's first president. In 1992, I was curator for an exhibition at the Michener Library, University of Northern Colorado. A new experience in 1993 was to be a juror for the Longmont Museum's annual quilt exhibition, A Stitch in Time.

Another change occurred in my life as a fiber artist when I returned to the university campus to complete my undergraduate degree. It was a challenge for several years, but very rewarding when I walked across the platform to receive a BFA, cum laude, in fiber with a minor in art history in May 1998 at Colorado State University.

In the fall of 1998, my husband and I moved to the rural community of Placitas, New Mexico. The dry desert landscape has changed my palette to one that represents sandy arroyos, eroded sandstone cliffs and remnants of deteriorated architectural forms. I continue to use cloth, but dyeing, piecing and quilting have evolved into painting, pasting and laminating the cloth onto wood panels. I remain linked to the traditions in making textiles as I seek the visual and textural elements of the landscape that influence the contemporary abstract expression of my work.

Tallahassee Lassie III

Tafi Brown
Alstead, New Hampshire
Joint Effort   63" x 63"   1992

Pieced cyanotype photographic prints on cotton using Kodalith negatives developed in both dektol and graphic arts developer. Cyanotype photographs of white pine boughs and hemlock. All photography done by artist; commercial cotton fabrics. Cotton batting. Machine pieced and quilted. This is a "Green Quilt."

This quilt was made two years after the raising of my own timber-frame home when I had returned to teaching art in the public schools. It is a visual record of the process of building my timber frame, including but not limited to the clearing of my land, the logging, kerfing, planing, raising and the frame itself. Many of the people—neighbors, friends, colleagues, students—without whose help I never would have been able to have my own house, are also included in my quilt. I built my house as close to an environmentally friendly house as I was able, and many of the trees used for timbers returned to be on the land where they grew.

Caryl Bryer Fallert
Paducah, Kentucky
Reflection #27   54" x 67"   1992

Hand-dyed cottons, hand printed, acrylic paints, tucking, machine pieced, machine quilted.

"For as long as I can remember, I have expressed myself through artwork. My formal training was primarily in design, drawing and studio painting. After many years of painting, sewing and experimenting with other media, I discovered that fabric, as an artistic medium, best expressed my personal vision.

I love the tactile qualities of cloth and the unlimited color range made possible by hand-dyeing, and other surface design techniques. Virtually all of my quilts begin with white, 100 percent cotton fabric. The fabric is dyed, painted and printed to create the palette of colors and visual texture used in piecing and appliquéing my images. In addition to continuing an ongoing series of colorful fantasy works, I have recently become very interested in images scanned and manipulated in the computer and printed directly on fabric with archival inkjet inks."

Caryl Bryer Fallert is internationally recognized for her award-winning art quilts, which are easily recognized by their luminous colors and illusions of light, depth and motion. Her attention to detail has earned her a reputation for meticulous craftsmanship as well as stunning designs.

Caryl is best known for her organic, curved-seam designs, including *Corona II: Solar Eclipse*, voted one of the one hundred best quilts of the twentieth century. In 2002, Caryl was selected as one of the thirty most influential quilt makers in the world. She is the only three-time winner of the coveted American Quilters Society Best of Show Purchase Award, and her quilts have won Best of Show in more than fifteen other national and international exhibitions. In addition, her quilts hang in museum, corporate, public and private collections throughout the world. Caryl's work has been exhibited extensively throughout North America, Europe and Japan, as well as New Zealand and Australia. She has had thirteen solo exhibitions in three countries. Her quilts have appeared in hundreds of national and international publications, including the covers of two Quilt National catalogs (1987 and 2001).

Born in 1947 in Elgin, Illinois, Caryl graduated with a BA from Wheaton College in 1969 and studied art at Illinois State University, College of DuPage, and University of Wisconsin. Caryl lives with her husband Bob in Paducah, Kentucky, where they are building a new studio and home.

Caryl finds her greatest joy designing and making her quilts and sharing what she has learned with students in her workshops and lectures, which have taken her to eleven countries on five continents.

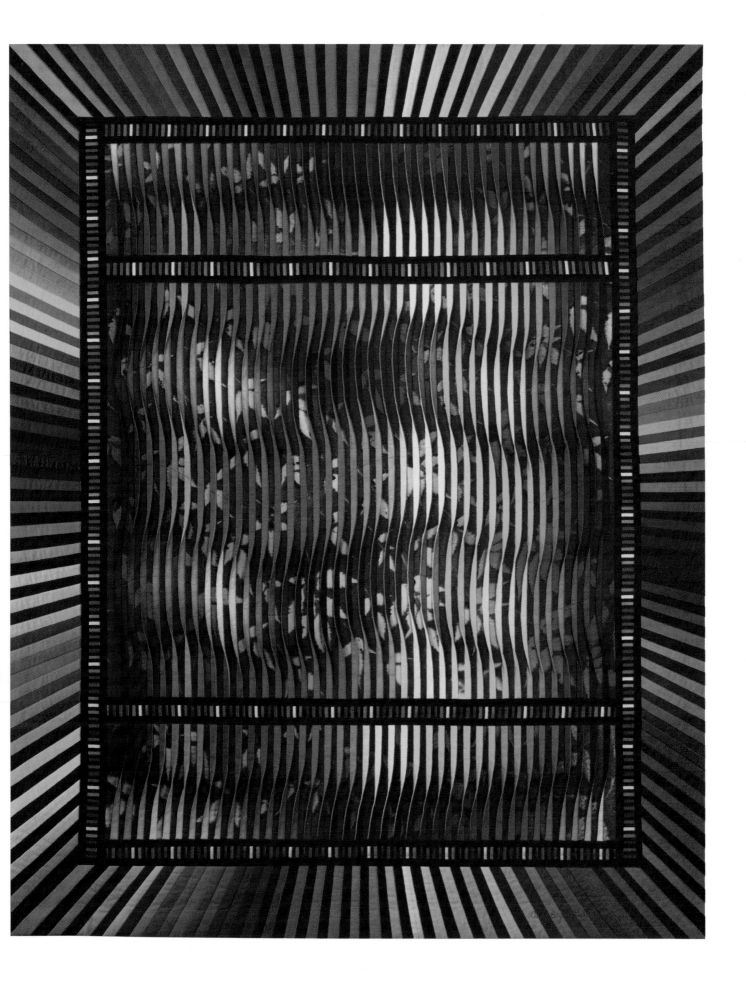

Patty Hawkins
Estes Park, Colorado
Road Blocks   67" x 76.5"   1992

Commercial cottons, machine pieced, machine quilted.

Growing up in Louisiana in the 1950s was an artistically stagnant time, however, my mother was a marvelous seamstress, teaching me the value of color and the intricacies of sewing. She emphatically told me "people say green and blue don't work well together," but she made them work anyway. We can certainly all point to the beauty of nature's color combinations.

With great encouragement from my family, I began watercolor painting thirty-five years ago when we moved to Colorado. The Denver Art Museum's exhibit, Craft: Poetry of the Physical in 1987, included work of contemporary quilt artists Nancy Crow, Michael James, Pam Studstill and Rise Nagin. It was monumental to realize quilts could be a much larger canvas to play on with color.

Life is a balancing act of giving time to family (three wonderful grandkids) and hikes with my husband in Rocky Mountain National Park. Being an artist is a gift that must be constantly practiced as well as shared in my classes teaching design and dye painting.

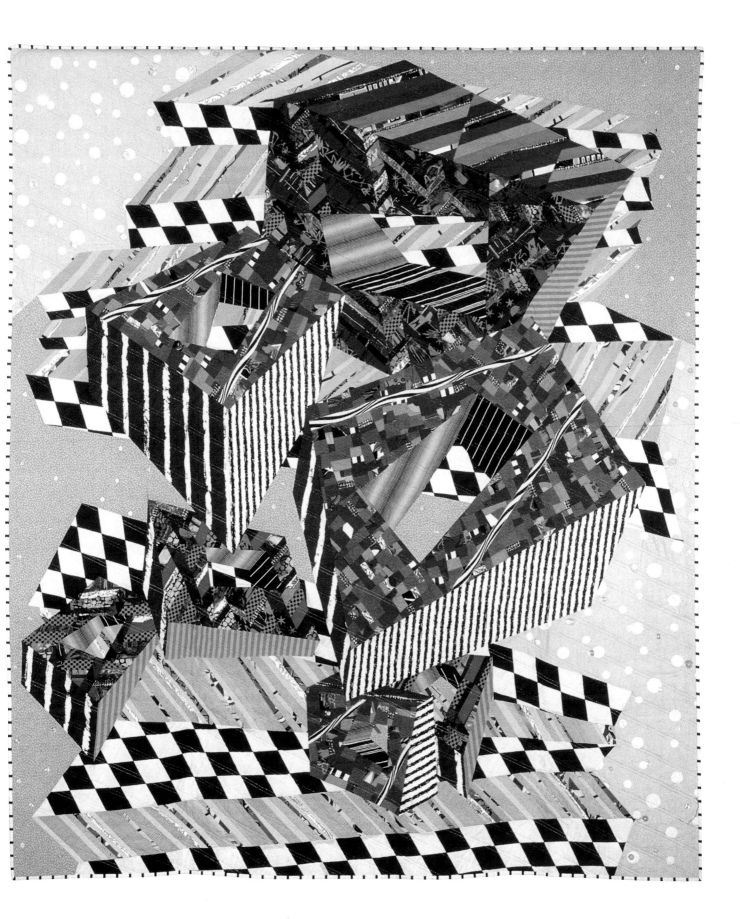

Mary Mashuta
Berkeley, California
Exploration: Learning to Get Along   71.5" x 70.5"   1992

Striped, Indian woven cottons, machine pieced, machine quilted.

I became a quiltmaker in the early '70s when quilters traced around cardboard templates and cut the pieces out by hand with scissors, before speed methods, special quilters' tools and quilters' fabrics were invented, before alternative methods of making quilts came into being, before there was such a thing as "art quilts."

By the '80s, I realized that my quilts could be a personal expression: art if you like. I learned to tell stories and make social commentary in fabric. However, to this day, I still enjoy a repeat block format and the "soft" feel of a traditionally made quilt.

My two college degrees were not in art, but I have had many art classes and worked in and taught interior design. I learned to make color and design choices long before I became a quilter (and others paid me to practice). Interior design work made me aware that commercial fabrics are printed or woven in multiple colorways (color versions of same design). *Exploration* was the first in a long series of multiple-colorway quilts.

I stirred the dye pots once and decided that my interest lies in searching out and accumulating fabric, not in making it. The process of putting together a special fabric collection is always enhanced by actually getting to use the fabrics in a quilt.

I support myself by writing about and teaching quiltmaking to people who want to make their quilts more innovative. I don't consider myself to be an art quilter, but rather a quiltmaker who sometimes gets to make serious art quilts. Much of the work I do has to be made accessible to the average quilter/reader. Often I work backward, or so it seems. A very serious piece like *Exploration* is created. Then simpler, more accessible versions follow.

I have discovered that I can make social commentary while making a quilt, but it doesn't have to be "in your face." If the viewer doesn't read my statement, they might never know what was in my mind as I worked on the quilt.

I made this quilt after I visited South Africa in the early '90s before the sanctions were lifted. The woven stripe fabrics purchased there seemed appropriate to use when

I wanted to create a quilt about the riots that followed the Rodney King verdict in South Central Los Angeles.

Here is part of my artist's statement from the time: *As I worked on this quilt, I realized how much getting to know the stripes I was working with was like getting to know people with whom we are unfamiliar. Whether the stripes were difficult or easy to work with, plain or fancy to look at, all of them contributed to the finished appearance of the quilt.*

It seems that mankind is still working on the issue of getting along and appreciating differences today.

Alison Schwabe
Montevideo, Uruguay
Ora Banda   59.5" x 49"   1992

Commercial cottons, hand dyed cottons, batiks, machine pieced, machine quilted.

As an early baby boomer, I was born in 1946. Like most Australian girls my age, I learned sewing and dressmaking at school to quite a high skill level. My mother and grandmothers embroidered counted-thread work, and my mother smocked large panels for dresses for her three daughters, making matching outfits for each season, until we grew old enough to rebel. I, too, sewed children's clothing and things for our home. A creative embroidery class in 1976 drew me to stitchery of all kinds. Since then I have been making and exhibiting nontraditional embroidered and quilted pieces.

Temporarily relocated to Colorado in 1987, I planned to study traditional American quilt making. The potential of the medium for personal designs and nontraditional techniques quickly became obvious, and by the late 1980s I began to create non-traditional quilted pieces. Landscape and man's activity within it has always been of interest to me—I majored in ancient history and geography. Inspired by man-made patterns painted, chipped or carved from cave walls, rocks and artifacts from the Southwest and the similarity to such markings from all other continents including my home, Australia, over several years I produced the Ancient Expressions series of quilts. Natural forces and the roles they play in shaping the natural landscape, inspired quilts such as *Undercurrents*, *Mission Beach*, *Desert Wind* and the bushfire and flood quilts of 1999–2001.

Since I began quiltmaking, I have used paint and dye in various ways, added beading and other embellishments, and no doubt will again. But underlying virtually all my designs is that enduring influence of American patchwork—the repeated block or unit, coupled with groups of inlaid strips. These units either stay irregularly shaped or are trimmed down to a square or triangle, since I very much like the juxtaposition of straight gridlines with wavy irregular lines. I first used strips as inserts but soon these strips became an important repeat element in my work, dividing major shapes. Initially set in formal patterns, (*Window onto Bougainvillea Street* and *Ora Banda*) softened in *Lilydale*, they began to wander irregularly. In their most recent development they have narrowed and themselves become irregularly shaped.

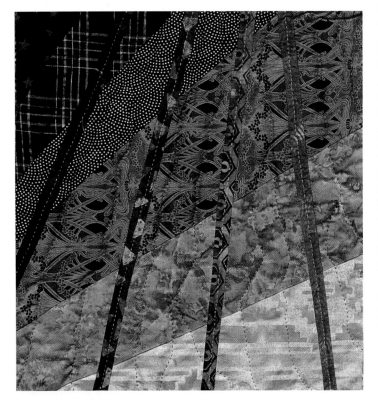

For personal reasons, most of my time is currently spent in Uruguay, South America. Here, fabrics are imported, expensive and not available in the huge ranges quiltmakers in Australia and North America are accustomed to accessing. I have brought both yardage and scraps with me from Australia on a number of trips back home and have plenty to keep me going for years here, something I think I have in common with many other quiltmakers. Here there are very few quiltmakers, and those I have met and the work they are doing have prompted my current quest to produce quilts paying closer attention to the frugal and thrifty origins of the craft, while maintaining my personal vision within each piece and the whole body of my work.

Diana Bunnell
Boulder, Colorado
Sewing Down the Bones   70" x 58"   1993

Hand-dyed and painted cottons, commercial cottons; machine pieced, raw edge appliqué, reverse applique, acrylic pearlized paints; cotton, wool and silk fibers, hand quilted, hand embellished.

I made my first quilt in 1978 when the art quilt movement was just emerging. At that time I had been a studio potter for many years.

My first quilts were a response to our beautiful Colorado landscape, including our Boulder landmark, the Flatirons. By combining quilting blocks, each depicting a different mood, I could express my appreciation for the constantly changing beauty of our mountains.

Influenced by my quilting friends I soon wanted to express more complex ideas in my work and to make it more uniquely my own. I experimented with the textural qualities of fabric by exposing raw edges, used acrylic paints to embellish the surfaces, dyed and discharged my own fabrics and incorporated computer-generated images. The possibilities, I found, were limitless.

Sewing Down the Bones was inspired by Natalie Goldberg's book *Writing Down the Bones* in which she encourages the reader to write spontaneously without editing. I decided to record my thoughts visually in fabric squares instead of words on paper. Then I assembled a number of the squares on a background of orange airbrushed canvas, attaching them with bold stitches and leaving raw edges. The three layers of the quilt are tied instead of quilted to emphasize the improvisational nature of the piece. This quilt was juried into Visions in 1994.

All of my quilts are autobiographical. They are my visual journal and, I hope, a record of my growth as an artist. As I continue, I want to edit less, play more and honor my own creativity.

"I recognize that improvisation allows for encounters of the finest kind." Eric Maisel

Terrie Hancock Mangat
Valdez, New Mexico
Desert Storm   85.5" x 95.5"   1993

Commercial cottons, reverse and hand appliqué, acrylic paints, small plastic skeletons, crushed toy cars, small plastic gas pumps.

Terrie Mangat is an internationally known textile artist who has been credited with pioneering and popularizing embellishment on contemporary quilts since the early 1970s. She graduated from the University of Kentucky in 1970 with a degree in art, and has exhibited and taught quilt making both in the United States and abroad for thirty years. Her work has been shown in many venues including the San Jose Quilt Museum, the Bernice Steinbaum Gallery in New York, the San Diego Historical Society and the International Folk Art Museum in Santa Fe. In 2000 her quilt, *Dashboard Saints: In Memory of Saint Christopher, Who Lost His Magnetism* was named one of the top one hundred American quilts of the twentieth century.

Mangat's quilts are mixed media and often depict something that she has seen or observed. Due to mastery of her technique, she is equally comfortable with pictorial, traditional or abstract expressions. The subject matter of her work generally falls into the categories of personal experience, social and political philosophy, and cultural and ethnographic appreciation. In addition to being a world-recognized quilt maker, She has created acclaimed designs for several commercial fabric houses. She also has constructed her own screen-printing studio where she practices the technical aspects of printing her hand-drawn gouache designs on silk and cotton.

Born and raised in Cold Spring, Kentucky, Terrie Hancock Mangat was heavily exposed to Kentucky's rich quiltmaking heritage, which formed her technical and aesthetic foundations for quiltmaking. She has been sewing by hand and machine since the age of six. She was inspired by Mrs. Earl B. Clay, and most of her quilts have been quilted by Sue Rule, both of Carlisle, Kentucky.

Following college, Terrie lived in Oklahoma with her husband and made her first visits to Santa Fe and Taos, New Mexico, places that would play an important role in her later work. During the '70s and '80s, Terrie traveled to Africa with her husband, who was born in Kenya. African cultural crafts and curios inspired her trademark use of beads, trinkets and other three-dimensional embellishments. Growing up near Cincinnati, which straddles the Mason-Dixon, Terrie gained a deep appreciation for Southern and Midwestern culture. This blend of American influences is most evident in her landmark quilt *American Heritage Flea Market.* Whether through an Elvis Presley lamp or an Uncle Sam coin bank, Terrie has always been intrigued by the cultural oddities that represent Americana. In 1994, Terrie and her sister, Becky

Hancock, founded St. Theresa Textile Trove in inner city Over-the-Rhine, Cincinnati. The store was not only a commercial enterprise but also an intersection of art, culture and service. Alongside the business, Terrie created after-school programs for latch-key children, providing an alternative to the perils of the street.

Terrie has lived in Taos, New Mexico, full-time since 1998.

Joan Schulze
Sunnyvale, California
Young Men and Chocolates   40" x 50"   1993

Paper, cotton fabrics, glue transfer images, metallic paints, machine quilted.

My early careers of elementary school teacher and mother of four are integral to the formation of my final vocation, artist, which was begun in earnest in 1970. I opted out of a formal study of art and worked at my own pace to acquire the photographic skills, textile techniques and mixed-media processes that would serve my ideas. My artistic practice gradually evolved yet always incorporated information and impressions from my life experiences. By 1974 I had found the quilt medium and never looked back.

In the studio I use collage thinking, which helps me transform disparate ideas, materials and other fragments that I hunt and gather, combine, recombine and change to create a new narrative.

Why do I use erasures, fragments and layering? For me they imply the passing of time. My glue transfer methods are slow, which encourages discovery of complex rhythms and stories. Image and text fragments relate to my love of photography, love of reading newspapers, magazines and books and being a poet. These sources provide many personal and unique to me fragments, especially in the rough drafts from my poems, which I love to juxtapose next to something strange and transforms its history. Appliqué dates from my early embroideries in the '70s. I often use it to add color or a dramatic line. A finished work may have peeled or eased area. Some do not. A technical necessity in making quilts, stitching to hold the layers together, also functions as a drawing—a risky mark-making act, not easily reversible as it leaves its own palimpsest.

I do think of my work in a literary way. Large quilts equate to the novel form, which requires time to decode. These constructions grace large public and private spaces. Medium-size quilts may be likened to short stories, often forming a series based on something I love such as the tea ceremony. My Haiku and Tank series of small works in paper and fabric are visual poems, reduced in size, rely on severe editing and are more meditative in feeling.

Not coming to quilts through a study of traditional sources and methods, I have worked as an improviser from quilt one. Now hundreds of quilts and thirty years later I still experiment and improvise. The excitement doesn't fade. I always look forward to another day in the studio, if—for nothing else— just to see what I will see.

Marta Amundson
Riverton, Wyoming
Please Stay By Me Diana   66" x 90"   1994

Cotton batiks, African fabrics, machine appliquéd, machine quilted.

Some people may not care what happens to a rare species of fish, a tiny bird from Hawaii or wolves as a part of the Yellowstone ecosystem. I care deeply, and my quilts reflect the various issues that concern me. Most recently, I want people to understand that I don't agree with the policies of the current administration and so I have alternately protested or poked fun at the government's actions via my art quilts. I also feel free to express the quirkier side of my personality with funny quilts about gender value in our society, my dreams, my amazing dog or iconic memories of my experiences.

My formal education lies in the fields of biology, ecology, visual art and art history. In the ten years before I was an art quilter, I made architectural stained glass for public buildings. The virtual light from within my quilts comes from my knowledge of the impact of light coming through glass. As an art historian I have experience with design elements and the rules of composition.

Since living on a ranch in Wyoming can be insular, I read voraciously. My world perception is shaped by Internet newspapers, television news and magazines. Teaching others about fiber art has given me the opportunity to travel and it is through my travels that I have been able to view firsthand the endangered animals that are the most typical subject matter for my quilts.

Most importantly, my work is subtle, tasteful, eye-catching and well crafted. My art quilts are seen first from a visual level and the inner agenda is not immediately clear. The viewer must exhibit curiosity and intelligence in order to enjoy the full impact of my visual statement. My goal is to make viewers smile and nod in an "ah-ha" moment, not tear their hair out. Women have more than a few opinions, and we are letting the public know about them. In the last thirty years, a medium that was traditionally viewed as women's craft has found its way into the art world.

Marta Amundson
Riverton, Wyoming
The New Holocaust   60" x 70"   1994

Cotton batiks, African fabrics, machine appliquéd, machine quilted.

Marta Amundson is a wildlife advocate and professional art quilter who exhibits throughout the United States and abroad. She writes a regular column for her guild newsletter in addition to articles on quilting for books and magazines in the United States, Australia and Britain. Known as the "quilting cowgirl," she teaches innovative machine quilting techniques around the world. Marta was chosen in 1995 and 2002 to receive the Wyoming Arts Council Fellowship and won the grand prize in the 2001 American Folk Art Museum International Competition. Her 128-page book *Quilted Animals* was published by the American Quilter's Society in June 2002. Her work is featured in the 2004 *Fiberarts Design Book 7*.

In addition to her passion for fly fishing, Marta is an avid skier. She also likes to kayak, bike and scuba dive. She often travels to exotic places to view and photograph endangered animals as inspiration for the drawings on her quilts.

Jane Dunnewold
San Antonio, Texas
Baby Quilt   36" x 45"   1994

Silk, synthetics, photo transfers, gold foil, birthday candles, machine stitched.

Although I have made quilts off and on for twenty years, I have never really thought of myself as a Quilter. My body of work has focussed on the whole cloth surface and my quilted pieces reflect that orientation. The stitching is never the important part of the piece.

I *have* always thought of myself as an artist, and cloth has always been my preferred medium. Most of my best work has had an emotional or psychological component. If I fit into "art quilt history" anywhere, it may be as an early champion of the quilt as personal story. My quilts and my cloth are vehicles for meditation, contemplation and working out. I solve personal dilemmas when I work, and making quilts has been an avenue to healing for me. Working as an artist, quiltmaker and teacher has allowed me to witness the healing and "opening" that can happen when a viewer relates to the artwork at hand. Knowing that my own life, expressed through my quilts, has touched someone else's life and perhaps even been helpful or inspiring is the greatest gift of artistic life.

Baby Quilt helped me work through mothering issues—the whole "single mother, not good enough, overwhelmed" crisis. But the amazing thing was that later it touched other women struggling with the same issues. Recognizing the ability a quilt has to be powerful proved to be an honor and a responsibility that continues to challenge me.

Wendy Huhn
Dexter, Oregon
Objects 2: Pasta   30.5" x 63.5"   1994

Photocopied black-and-white images on colored cotton fabrics, machine pieced, machine quilted.

I am: a collector of skeletons, heart-shaped rocks, ephemera, dolls, license plates, religious icons and books—tons of books. I am: a visual scavenger of imagery. I borrow imagery from nineteenth- and twentieth-century magazines and books to alter and reconstruct. I am: a storyteller. The stories I tell through my work reflect the way I view the world—often a brash voice in a room of hushed tones. My sometimes controversial textiles arise more from conviction than contrariness. How one might interpret my work is, of course, unquestionably personal.

As a child I was obsessed with creating my own paper dolls. I would cut and paste together my own creations from magazines, often using the forbidden *Playboy*, which I found in dumpsters. To buy commercially printed male paper dolls in the late 1950s was a rarity. I would reassemble the pieces to create my own paper people. This is how I continue to work, scavenging, cutting, pasting, enlarging, reducing and waiting for the work to sing.

I've been working with textiles professionally since 1983. I received my BFA in fibers from the University of Oregon in 1980. I don't consider myself a quilter— I prefer the label of mixed-media artist. I will employ whatever technique and use whatever medium that lends itself best to the project I'm working on. *Objects 2: Pasta* is part of a long series of using found objects and my photocopier, Igor, to "print" the image directly on fabric. Simple but effective. I was interested in the dimensional depth that can only be achieved by using this process.

My work has evolved over the years from using the photocopier to print directly on the fabric to currently painting on canvas and making small embroidered work.

Dominie Nash
Bethesda, Maryland
Peculiar Poetry 10   44.5" x 44.5"   1994

Hand-dyed cottons, silks, machine pieced and raw edge appliqué, machine quilted.

I am a full-time studio art quilter, primarily self-taught. From the start of my quilting career more than twenty years ago, I have dyed and printed all the fabrics used in my collage-like quilts. After a brief career in social work, I discovered the textile arts in the late 1960s and began to explore as many techniques and materials as I could, making mostly functional objects. I felt I had finally found a kind of work that would be fulfilling over the long haul. At the beginning I concentrated on weaving and dyeing, making a few quilts now and then. The number kept increasing until I realized that this was my medium. I didn't know many quilters or see many art quilts, so I gradually developed my own way of doing things (often incorrectly) and a personal style, which involved finding a way to do the types of designs I envisioned while bypassing my inability to be precise. Hence, a sort of overlapping appliqué, leaving the edges raw, was my solution. Since I didn't know the rules, I was free to break them and to achieve the kind of spontaneity I was seeking.

After working at home for a number of years, I moved to a studio in a school and then to my current location in an artists' co-op. Although I had taken my work seriously from the beginning, working in the studio was the final step I needed to consider myself an artist. I saw many changes in my quilts and began to develop a consistent body of work and learn more surface design processes, one of my favorite aspects of my work. I began exhibiting in more national fiber, quilt and mixed-media shows, and my work appeared in many publications.

I have always felt that my work defied categorization in the art quilt movement, but the acceptance both in exhibits and in the community as a whole has kept me identified with it. I have made more than 150 quilts and have many more to go. Some are planned in detail; others grow from a dropcloth or other piece of found fabric. I have worked abstractly for most of my career and am currently exploring representational work in my still life series. No matter where the next quilts take me, I can't imagine being without the opportunity to start with plain, white cloth and end up with an expression of my feelings and ideas. There are so many opportunities for growth and change that, though sometimes frustrated, I am never bored.

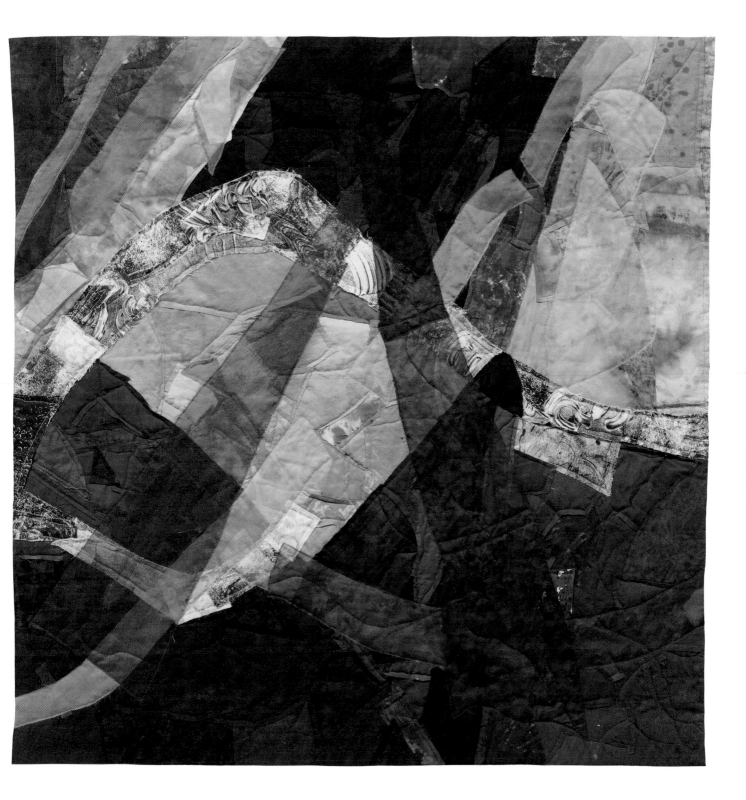

Judith Tomlinson Trager
Boulder, Colorado
Abstraction/Diffraction   53" x 54"   1994

Hand-dyed fabrics, commercial fabrics, metallic paints, machine pieced, machine quilted.

My quilts reflect the light around me. They grow from the landscape of the West and seek to incorporate the diversity of place. Color, movement, texture and sometimes history blend together to create dense surfaces and flowing lines. I try to evoke a mood and sense of memory with my quilts by the use of color and patterning. My work tells stories that only the careful viewer can interpret.

Nancy Erickson
Missoula, Montana
Hand Shadows   59" x 61.5"   1995

Cotton canvas, commercial fabrics, acrylic paints, machine pieced, machine quilted.

Almost all of my life I have been an artist. After acquiring degrees in zoology and foods and nutrition, I realized that what I really wanted to do was to make art, so I returned to school and received an MA and an MFA in painting and drawing.

I've been making quilts since 1975, when I made a flat velvet piece with big stuffed hoops on it and a large purple cat prowling through it all. This piece was a combination of sculpture and quilting, and from there I went on to large wall pieces, also with stuffed elements, and finally to flat, machine quilted works of velvet, cotton and satin. I've made variations of the flat fabric work up to the present time: I stuffed my last tree in the *Pattee Canyon Fire* quilt in 1978, saying to myself, "I've got to find a simpler way to get these ideas out."

In the '80s I introduced the human form in my piece *The Goddess and the Capybara*, and I continued with combinations of the human with capybaras (the world's largest rodent), rabbits (we had a house rabbit), and lions. Gradually the pieces assumed a house shape, then a tilted house shape, and finally only the essential elements were included in the quilt: A lion on stairs with an old light bulb and fires would constitute the whole quilt.

Since the 1980s I have been using the environmental themes of war and destruction. With the inception of the Gulf War, I spent a year and a half just drawing bears, a favorite subject since childhood stories of the Far North held me entranced, with oil paint sticks, a new medium for me. In the '90s I returned to fabric with the idea of working differently, more like the paintings. This resulted in a long series of works featuring bears taking over the artist's studio, taking back some of the territory humans have stolen. The painting, *Hand Shadows*, is one of these quilts, a community of individuals playing simple, creative games, making the best of a situation that is dangerous outside.

Reading books about the cave paintings in France, especially Lascaux and Chauvet, led to another series, the Hall of Memory quilts. These works were ongoing through the end of the 1990s.

In all these years, absolutely nothing else has been as challenging or as satisfying as drawing, painting and working in fabric. Right now I'm making cutout works in velvet of cave drawing symbols, stitched, painted, and appliquéd on the surface of large cougars, and most recently, humans. These form an environment on the wall, perhaps somewhat like a cave. The recent work is more pacific, more related to the gesture of the cougars, more concerned with their pattern on the wall.

Sally Sellers
Vancouver, Washington
Volume One   40" x 46"   1995

Commercial fabrics, hand-dyed cottons, silks, synthetics, decorative threads, couching, raw edge machine appliqué, machine quilted.

As long as I can remember, I have loved to make things. It is part and parcel of who I am. Having the ability to draw accurately was my definition of an artist; since I cannot, I never considered myself to be in that category until much later in life. Regardless of the label, I have always experienced unparalleled joy when creating things.

I began making quilts in 1989 when corporate downsizing forced me to rechannel my obsessive tendencies from data processing into textiles. Quilts were geometric, cloth was familiar and the combination of the two proved greatly rewarding. Once exposed to nontraditional quilts at the Oregon College of Arts and Crafts, I very quickly embraced the genre now known as Art Quilts.

My work is best characterized by a love of pattern and a disdain for (or inability to create) a straight line. In the 1990s, I frequently used the house shape, which I love for its inherent emotional context as well as its geometrical joy. Grids are implied or openly present in much of my work. They are immensely appealing to me. With their processions of discrete entities or images, they offer the illusion that the world can be categorized, understood and therefore controlled, a fallacy I continue to employ until this very day.

Although initially adverse to detailed handwork, in the last few years I have been embellishing my work with beads in addition to discarded mechanical and electronic components. Like many before me, I now look at all small objects with an eye for their design possibilities. Few things are allowed to be thrown away. I have recently enlarged my studio.

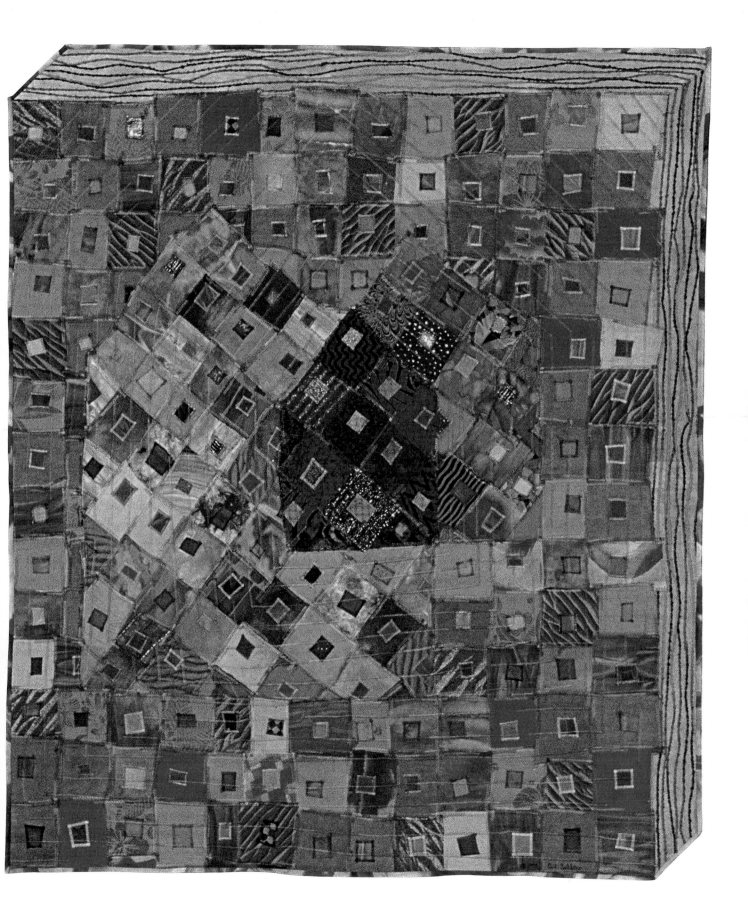

Carole Lyles Shaw
Laurel, Maryland
African Dreams—A Collaboration Quilt   35.5" x 39.5"   1995

African batik fabrics. Embellished with beads, shell and bone objects, machine pieced and quilted.

Carole was invited to exhibit seven art quilts from her Pentecostal Cross Quilts series at the Virginia Quilt Museum in Summer 2001. Carole's work has also been juried into Contemporary Works of Faith '95 the Liturgical Art Guild of Ohio's 14th Biennial International Exhibition, and Women In the Visual Arts, Erector Square Gallery, New Haven, Connecticut. She was invited to give a special presentation at the Renwick Gallery of the Smithsonian Institution in late 2000. Her talk, "Celebrating the Divine: Spirituality and Cultural Memory in African American Art Quilts," was part of Comfort and Joy: Quilting Community, Memory and Spirit, a symposium conducted in conjunction with the exhibit Spirits of the Cloth: Contemporary Quilts by African American Artists.

Her work appears in several publications including *Spirits of the Cloth* by Carolyn L. Mazloomi; *American Quiltmaking, 1970-2000* by Eleanor Levie; *The Art Quilt* and *Quilts Today: A Living Tradition* by Robert Shaw; and *Great Patchwork: Working With Squares and Triangles* by Eleanor Levie.

Carole is the author of two articles: "African American Artquilters" (*Surface Design Journal*) and "Inspiration From the Spirit" (*American Quilter*). She is one of the artists featured in *Creativity: Touching the Divine*, a documentary film cosponsored by ABC-TV and the U.S. Catholic Conference that has appeared on national television.

Carole is founder and president of the Columbia Resource Group, a management consulting firm working in leadership development, team building and organizational change. Her clients include the World Bank, Goddard Space Flight Center, the Potomac Electric Power Company (PEPCO) and many other companies and federal government agencies.

Fran Skiles
Plantation, Florida
Thread Bare II   54.5" x 52"   1995

Cotton canvas, rug hooking mesh ground, tulle, yarn, buttons, monofilament, flat braid, acrylics, gel medium transfers, machine pieced (raw-edge appliqué), machine quilted.

Creating art excites me! It is my passion. The thrill of discovery is the fuel that drives my engine; wondering what my constructions will look like during their development—and upon their completion. Sort of like fishing yet better.

In the 1980s I remember getting my first glimpse at this new art form—the Art Quilt. I discovered a book called *The Contemporary Quilt*, published in 1978. Pouring over it from cover to cover I found myself thinking, "This is where I belong". The quilts notably featured in this book were by artists Molly Upton, Clara Wainswright and Radka Donnell. Each quilt in the book was a stunning example of extraordinary work, and each quilt gave me validation that the strict rules of traditional quilting need not apply.

My path to art quilting began in the late 1970s when I began producing and selling framed, pieced fabric collages. In 1990, I enlarged these constructions and added finishing work to make them art quilts. The transition from small collages to large free-hanging collages was a natural evolution.

I've had a love affair with fabric my whole life. As a child, I was raised in a home that honored all types of sewing, from embroidery to machine work. My degree is a BA in home economics with a minor in art. As a practicing artist my philosophy is that fabric must work for me. I use untreated silk and cotton duck from the bolt. In the deconstruction and construction process of creating an art quilt, I cut, tear, sew, bond and paint fabric. I am told that I destroy the hand of the fabric and that is certainly true. I build a complex surface that reflects my interest in nature. I interpret what I see around me into shapes that become abstract. My work has been called an imaginary landscape. I want my work to contain mystery and struggle,

and this takes time. There is a lot of backward and sideways movement. I like to bring designs to a point of being out of control and then bring them back again.

Photography plays a major part in the content and design of my work. The images are taken and manipulated by me and come mostly from rural central Florida. The photography is transferred to fabric using photo silkscreen, heat-set transfer paper, acrylic emulsion lift and inkjet printing.

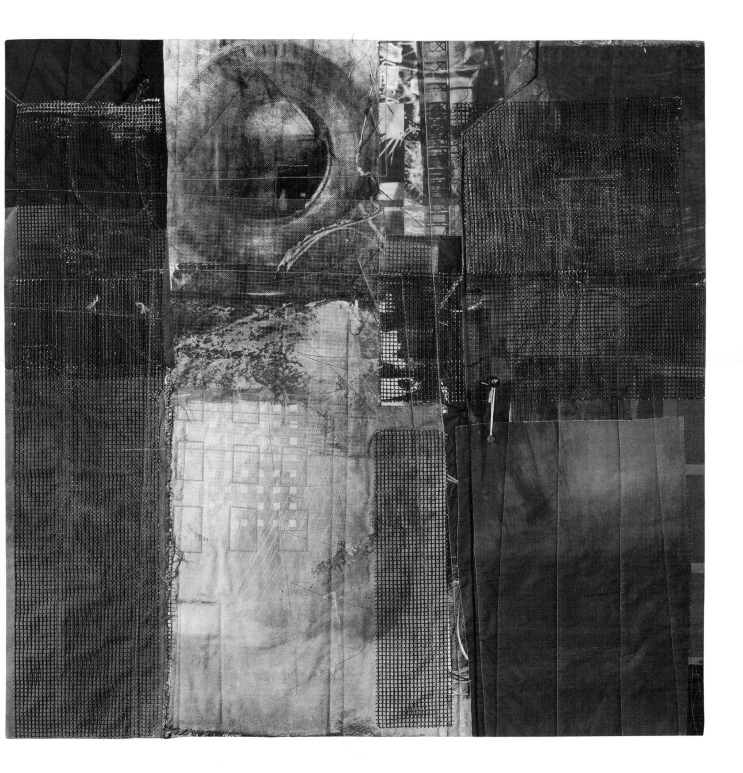

Katy Widger
Edgewood, New Mexico
Diamond Cross Square 49" x 49" 1995

Hand-dyed fabrics, handmade stamped images in black acrylic, machine pieced, machine quilted.

"My fiber work deals primarily with shapes formed by light and shadow, and texture inherent in earth, water and sky. When pursuing an idea, my working process is collage: gluing, layering and juxtaposing shapes, colors, textures. The Source of my images is the power and majesty evident in the landscape, the cosmos, the dance of life around us and my response of awe and gratitude. My creative process is a private conversation, immersed in serendipity that transforms dye, paint, fabric and thread into lyrical images of color, texture and form."

Katy Widger is a fourth-generation New Mexican, descended from historical Texas and New Mexico pioneers. She was raised in the small rural village of Corrales, north of Albuquerque, and focused on fine arts in high school. Remembering the quilts her grandmothers had made, she constructed her first quilt while snowbound for two weeks on a remote cattle ranch in central New Mexico in the late 1970s. It was then she realized the potential quilt making held as an art form and determined that it would become hers. She pursued a fine arts major at San Juan College, concentrating on color theory and design, and began dyeing, painting and printing her own fabric. Her work quickly became known for its rich intuitive color, the harmony of diverse textures and shapes and superb craftsmanship. She continues to be enchanted by the magic of changing white fabric into exquisite colors and textures, creating the surface design that becomes part of the contemplative and spiritual expression in her art. Now a master in the art of hand-dyeing fabric, Katy has shared this expertise and knowledge with many thousands in her self-published book, *Color Wheel Fabric Dyeing*, which continues to be in demand.

During the twenty years Katy has been creating art quilts her style and focus have evolved from purely geometric color studies to lyrical abstract imagery and recently, more classically representational work. She credits this journey with her ongoing study of fine art and her desire to create work that is highly personal and removed from what is generally considered traditional quilt making. Drawing, painting and art history have remained a lifelong pursuit. She is currently studying oil painting on canvas with a private teacher.

Ann Johnston
Lake Oswego, Oregon
Shock Waves 45.5" x 40.5" 1996

Monoprinted fabric, hand-dyed fabrics, machine pieced, machine quilted.

Shock Waves came from the images embedded (accidentally) in the fabric I dyed. When I cut, pieced, quilted and dyed it again, I did have a specific idea in mind, but I do not want to limit the meanings of the quilt by defining them. I enjoy knowing that it may mean something very different to another viewer, and I regret that I do not get to hear more often what that meaning may be.

The fabric I used in *Shock Waves* was the result of exploring large-scale monoprinting with thickened dyes and one of my early uses of dye to overpaint parts of the design after quilting and binding the piece. I don't know of anyone in 1996 who was doing either of these things in their quilts. Now, in 2004, I have finished another *Shock Wave* quilt. Even though it looks nothing like the first, it came from the same sense of movement and reaction.

First, my grandmother taught me to sew, then I learned to dye fabric. In between, I earned a BA in literature, married Jim, worked for Peace Corps Peru, started my first quilt, earned an MA in geography, had two sons and got hooked on quilting. By now, I have been making quilts and putting dye on fabric for over thirty years. My years of experimentation have led to mountains of hand-dyed fabric and quilts, thousands of miles of travel, numerous shows and exhibitions, four books and many, many friends.

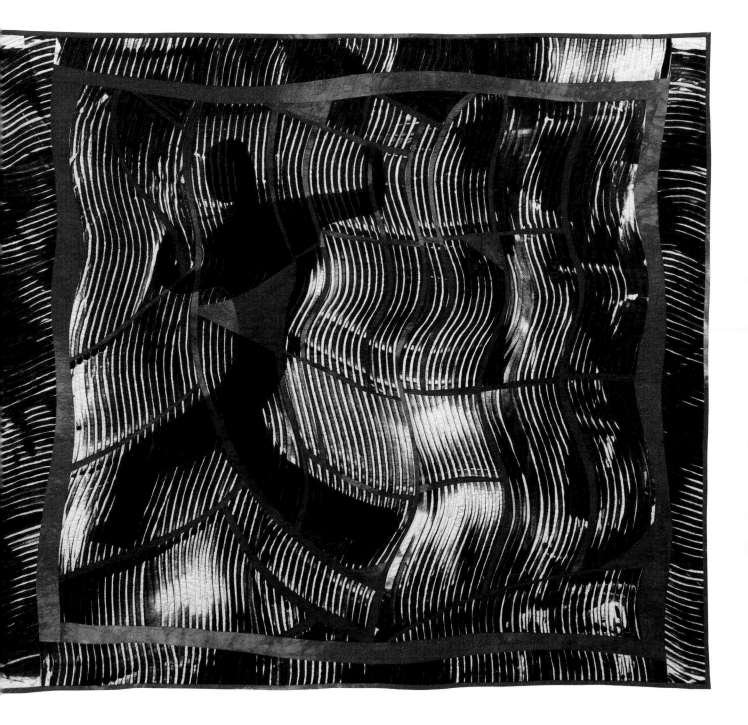

Lynda MH Faires
Louisville, Colorado
Tessera (Tiles)   73" x 73"   1997

Hand-dyed cottons, machine pieced, machine quilted with variegated threads.

Reflecting memories of tiles and mosaics in cathedrals, mosques, temples and castles of the world, *Tessera* began with the intention of creating a contemporary improvisational quilt based on a traditional pattern, the square in a square. I started with a selection of hand-dyed fabrics in an earthtone palette and created each block individually, paying attention only to the composition in terms of fabric, color and contrast choices. After completing several blocks, I began to arrange them on my design wall, looking for good overall composition and counterplay. One day a gust of wind blew all the blocks down from my design wall. I interpreted this event as a sign that I was composing too ridgidly and started over with a much less structured attitude, leaving various areas of the composition open as blocks of solid color. This quilt intrigues the eye of the viewer into looking deep into the surface in search of a logical pattern, which hopefully will not be found.

I grew up sewing, learning from my grandmother so young that I do not remember learning. My great aunts were quilters, and I slept under their quilts. I sewed my own clothes through college and my daughter's clothes when she was young. My professional career has alternated in long cycles between science and art, and I returned to school at age thirty-three for a PhD in chemistry, thinking I was finished with sewing. Ten years later, in the midst of a successful scientific career, sewing slipped unexpectedly back into my life when my grandmother passed away and much of her furniture and spirit moved into my house. Within three years, I had retired from science and made a quantum leap into my new avocation: art quilts, wearables and teaching.

From the beginning, I had a strong affinity for creating art wearables, especially very extravagant runway pieces that make metaphorical statements. I have designed

for the Fairfield and Bernina fashion shows. I have spent many months in Europe and studied machine embroidery with several outstanding English embroiderers. I love fabrics of all kinds, especially silks, velvets, linens and beautiful weaves like ikats. When traveling, I collect fabrics, linens, lace, trim, beads and buttons, old and new. I seek out European flea markets and love the thrill of the treasure hunt. My studio is a treasure trove of years of collecting.

After years of alternating between the two, I now feel my science mind and my artist mind work together. With my computer connected to my state-of-the-art embroidery-sewing machine, I can create my own designs digitally and control all aspects of the stitched design from the technical to the aesthetic. I am working now in multimedia collage, using rich embellished and embroidered materials to create lavish surfaces. Besides creative sewing and world travel, my passions include gardening, photography, my mountain cabin, my daughter and two grandsons.

Gretchen B. Hill
Longmont, Colorado
Looking West   62" x 19.5"   1997

Hand-dyed fabrics, machine pieced, machine quilted.

I love the interplay between colors of different hues and intensities. Nature has always been an inspiration for both my designs and color choices. The surprises I receive when I dye my own fabrics are amazing. I often paint, stamp and change the fabric in other ways to enhance the look I wish to achieve. Piecing, appliquéing and quilting bring another dimension to these beautiful fabrics.

I was born in Philadelphia, Pennsylvania, but grew up in Bethesda, Maryland. My father was an MD and a research scientist with National Institutes of Health, and my mother was trained as a nurse. The weekends were filled with gardening.

This, along with summer camp in the Pocono Mountains, gave me a love of nature and its wonderful colors and designs.

I majored in biology in college, but never pursued a career in it. After marrying, I had three little girls who inspired me to sharpen my sewing skills. Quilting was a natural progression with all the scraps from their outfits. I began as a traditional quilter around the time of the Bicentennial of our country. Quickly, I tired of the repetition and wanted more of a challenge. Because our family moved often, thanks to IBM, I began design groups wherever we lived, bringing art quilters together. In 1989 I helped found Front Range Contemporary Quilters in Colorado.

Linda Levin
Wayland, Massachusetts
Mangrove II 37.5" x 33.5" 1997

Hand-dyed synthetics, sheer overlays, machine appliquéd (raw-edge), machine quilted.

This piece was inspired by kayak trips through the mangrove swamps in Florida. The tangle of tree roots and lush foliage reflected in the smooth, unruffled surface of the water led me to use transfer-dyeing and other techniques to render the exciting images they evoked.

Mangrove II was made with synthetic fabrics primarily, dyed by me, and assembled in a collage-like manner. Sheer overlays and dense areas of stitching were also used to heighten and define certain areas.

After graduating from art school, marrying and raising four children, I discovered through a series of happy accidents and some strange coincidences that dyeing and sewing fabric suited me better than paint and canvas. In the more than twenty years since I began, I've learned, experimented, learned some more and have begun to see where my strengths and weaknesses lie.

I find my inspiration comes from my immediate surroundings in tiny glimpses that get very freely interpreted. Since I spend the larger part of my time in a woodsy suburb and the rest in New York, there is no shortage of exciting moments. Although I spend my time taking large pieces of fabric, reducing them to rags and laboriously reassembling them, my career on the basketball court has brought me equal fame and, dare I say it, fortune. Shown here, I am practicing with a junior member of my team, "The Dribblers." Our record this year is 17–2, a fact of which we are justifiably proud. Our senior division, "The Glorious Grannies," all wearing our hand-sewn shibori ensembles with matching Nikes, is the envy of all who see us.

Patty Hawkins
Estes Park, Colorado
Reflections #3   56" x 57"   1998

Hand-dyed and silk-screened cottons, machine pieced, machine quilted.

Having worked in the watercolor medium, Cezanne's quote says what I strive to accomplish in quilting: "There are no contrasts of light and dark, but the contrasts given by the sensation of color. When colors are harmoniously juxtaposed and complete, the picture develops modeling of its own accord." (*Cezanne, Father of 20th Century Art*, Abrams, 1994.)

Color is my foremost emphasis in working. My hand-dyed fabrics give me opportunity to work with many value contrasts, while keeping to a minimal color range. Recent works were fragmented color washes, creating a mood or season of the year. Living in Colorado has influenced me to create abstract mountain landscapes and skyscapes. Mesa Verde's Anasazi cliff dwellings literally punctuated my need to work in one color, using many values to make the visual texture of stone work.

Presently my work is fabric collages/montages, described as fragments of ideas or influences, brought together for visual impact, as witnessed in my infatuation of the "scribbles" seen in skyscraper windows. I am now creating with my shibori-dyed fabrics nature's strong influence in aspen trees, streams and river rocks. Personal stitchery marks are applied for visual texture.

My eyes are constantly searching for new motifs and patterns everywhere. This is also the theme of my teaching and lecturing. Art can be most powerful. I encourage viewers to see things with new eyes, and demanding more thought is exciting to me.

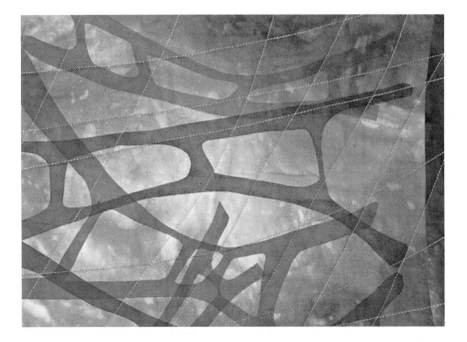

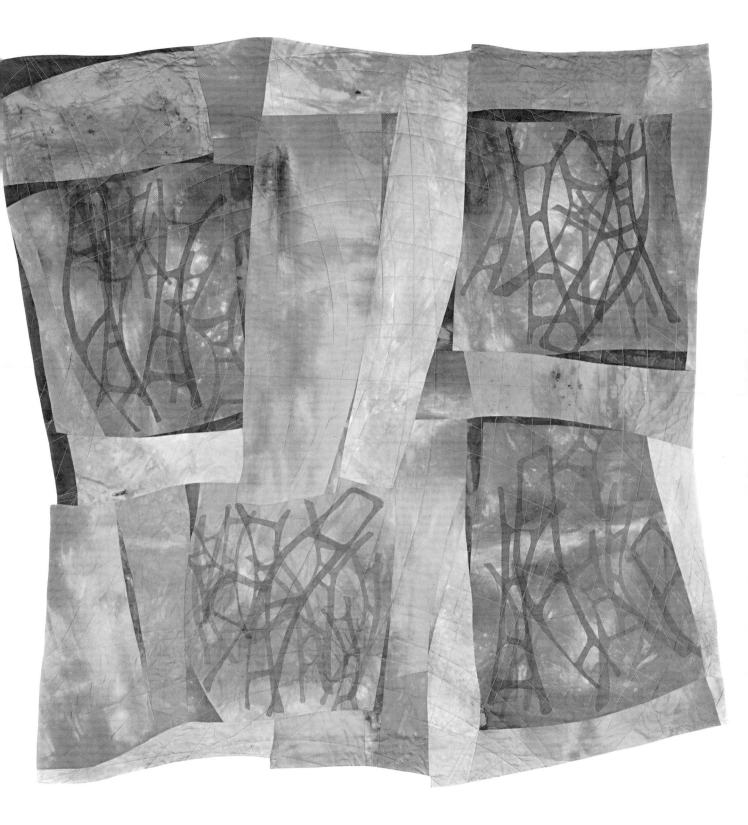

Ellen Oppenheimer
Oakland, California
T Block #4   47" x 47"   1998

Hand-silk-screen-printed and overdyed cottons, machine pieced, machine quilted.

I began to work with textiles over thirty years ago. Initially I made quilts that were variations on patterns from Pennsylvania Dutch and Amish quilt traditions. From those historically inspired quilts my work evolved into a very contemporary and geometric expression. In the last decade I have begun to explore traditional quilt patterns again but with all the knowledge and skills that decades of work have developed. I use both textile dyes and inks to print squares of fabric that I sew together to make variations on traditional quilt patterns. The essential structure of my work is based on a series of very simple patterns that result in a multifaceted masterpiece of geometry and color.

The geometry and patterns of quilts has always been very compelling and fascinating to me. Within this context I am exploring a balance of color, line and form. I am also able to refer to historical or traditional textiles. Ideally my quilts represent a logical and chronological progression of the history of traditional American quilts. I want these pieces to resemble and suggest traditional, woven or embroidered textiles from all over the world. I want them to be essentially "textile" while they are still quilts.

Caterpillars that were raised in my son's kindergarten class inspired the colors and patterns in this quilt. The teachers raised Luna moths, which develop from neon green caterpillars with orange and red accents, that grow larger than a person's finger. The moths are a lovely soft green color when they emerge and look more like a work of art than an insect. We also raised anise swallowtail butterflies, whose caterpillars are also green but have detailed patterns in black and orange. The brilliant and extravagant colors of these insects were fascinating to me and influenced my work for several years.

My son's school also influenced me to begin to work as an artist in residence in public elementary schools. As a community artist I have taught and worked with all age groups from preschool to senior citizens. Working with the support of numerous grants I have been in over one hundred different classrooms and have worked with thousands of students. Work my students completed while I was an artist in residence at Peralta Elementary School is permanently installed in many public buildings, including the American embassy in Moscow. I also worked on a grant from the Creative Work Fund to make quilts and banners with Oakland Elementary School students for installation in public libraries.

My work is well represented in museum and private collections. Both the Renwick and the American Museum of Art and Design have important quilts of mine in their collection. The Oakland Museum of California also has a quilt in their collection. In 1992 I was awarded a Western States National Endowment of the Arts Regional Fellowship. I have also received grants from many public and private institutions. I was recently honored by the International Quilt Association by having my work included in the twentieth century's best American quilts.

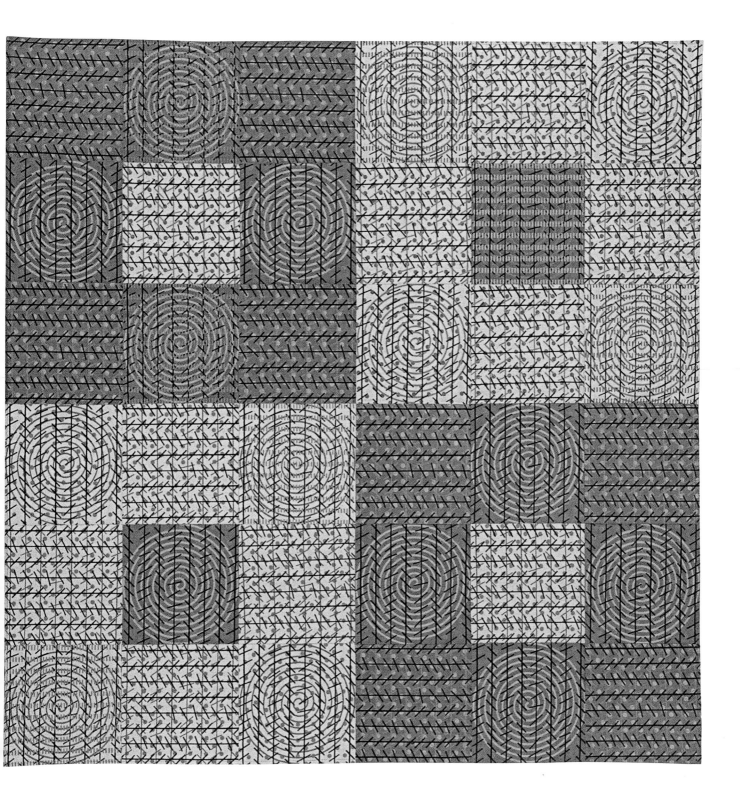

Sandra Sider
Bronx, New York
Infrastructure   41.5" x 32"   1998

Hand-screened and painted cottons, synthetics. Hand-dyed fabrics, gel emulsion transfer images, acrylics, metallic paints, rayon binding. Machine pieced, regular and reverse appliqué, hand and machine quilted.

Born in Alabama in 1949, I was raised in western North Carolina in a family of longtime Appalachian quilt makers. HGTV's *Simply Quilts* program is currently featuring the relationship of my work to this Appalachian heritage. After moving to New York City in 1979, I began to combine photographic techniques, especially cyanotype and photo transfer, with machine-quilted constructions.

My work was influenced by some of the alternative materials and processes used by artists in the women's movement. Since the mid-1980s, most of my work has focused on art quilts incorporating photography, as I have personalized and developed various approaches to images in textile assemblage. Formal training in studio art has been via classes and workshops at the School of Visual Arts and Manhattan Graphics Center.

My art quilts are in several public and private collections; they have been published nationally in books and art journals. My essays on American fiber art usually are published in *Fiberarts* magazine. An interview with New York artist Tom Fruin, who creates quiltlike structures, recently appeared in *Surface Design Journal*. I am a member of Studio Art Quilt Associates, Manhattan Quilters Guild, Art Quilt Network/ New York, the Surface Design Association, Friends of Fiber Art International, and the College Art Association. My current book in progress, *Quilts and Art: 1960 to 1980*, discusses the work of twenty-nine contemporary American quilt artists. I am also a PhD candidate at the Institute of Fine Arts, New York University, and have taught art history at Fordham University and the City College of New York.

Sylvia H. Einstein
Belmont, Massachusetts
Requiem for an Ashtree   40" x 40"   1999

Commercial fabrics, machine pieced, machine quilted.

I was working on *Requiem for an Ashtree* when they took down an old, magnificent tree next to our house. Both great trees and quilts are for me a symbol of the resilience of the human spirit.

I love the unexpected discoveries in crazy piecing, a technique that you can never quite control. I use commercially printed fabrics; in this quilt they were Marimekko scraps, an African print and a very contemporary fabric. I like arranging scraps, found materials of someone else's design, into a new form. I collage with printed, eccentric fabric, and out of this dialogue with the material comes the finished quilt.

Born and educated in Switzerland I came to the United States in 1965. I have always loved textiles and took classes in many techniques. When the Boston Center for the Arts announced a quilt show in 1975, I bought a book by Jean Ray Laury and made my first quilt, an appliquéd flag tree in red, white and blue with hand quilting, machine quilting and tying. I fell in love with quilts and took classes. This was a time of great excitement: there were few rules, little available information, and every quilt was an experiment. I discovered the Quilters Connection, an adventurous group with Nancy Halpern, Ruth McDowell and Rhoda Cohen. We used to travel great distances to see a quilt show or hear a speaker, once four hours (each way) to listen to Jean Ray Laury, one of my heroes.

In the early '70s I exhibited in group shows at the Brockton Art Center and the Danforth Museum, and in 1986 I was accepted in the 2nd Quilt Biennale in Heidelberg, Germany. After that show I was able to teach in Europe every year. I had also found my own style.

I have no art background; I was a medical technician and then a full-time mother. I have taken many classes, not only in quilting but also in museums and art schools. My first color class was very basic and wonderful. I am a member of two critique groups and give credit to my colleagues for encouragement and technical help. None of us work in the same style, but we have influenced each other. We also share information on shows and occasionally exhibit together.

I have had several successful one-person shows in Switzerland and in New England, and in 2005 I will exhibit in the Einbeck, Germany, museum, and have been accepted to my fifth Quilt National. My work is published in many magazines, catalogs and books in several languages. It is wonderful to be part of the quilt renaissance and to see the growth of art quilts.

Debra Lunn and Michael Mrowka
Lancaster, Ohio
Terrazzo: Lapis 28" x 27.5" 1999

Hand-dyed shibori cottons, fused, machine quilted.

We are fascinated by the magical quirks that we have been able to discover in various dye and discharge techniques. We discover some of these quirks intentionally by playing like "scientists," doing controlled experiments and taking notes. Others are happy accidents—gifts from the universe.

To produce the fabrics for our shibori series of quilts, we use a modernized version of an ancient Japanese pole-wrap technique. We wrap hundreds of quarter yard pieces of fabric on poles and dye them multiple times to achieve the colors we want. These fabrics have a "voice" of their own, and our job is to work with them in a way that allows them to speak.

Our quilts are a collaboration; we discuss the process and the results at every juncture even though our roles in the act of creating are different. For our shibori (tie-dye) series, Debra ties and Michael dyes. Both design and Debra sews.

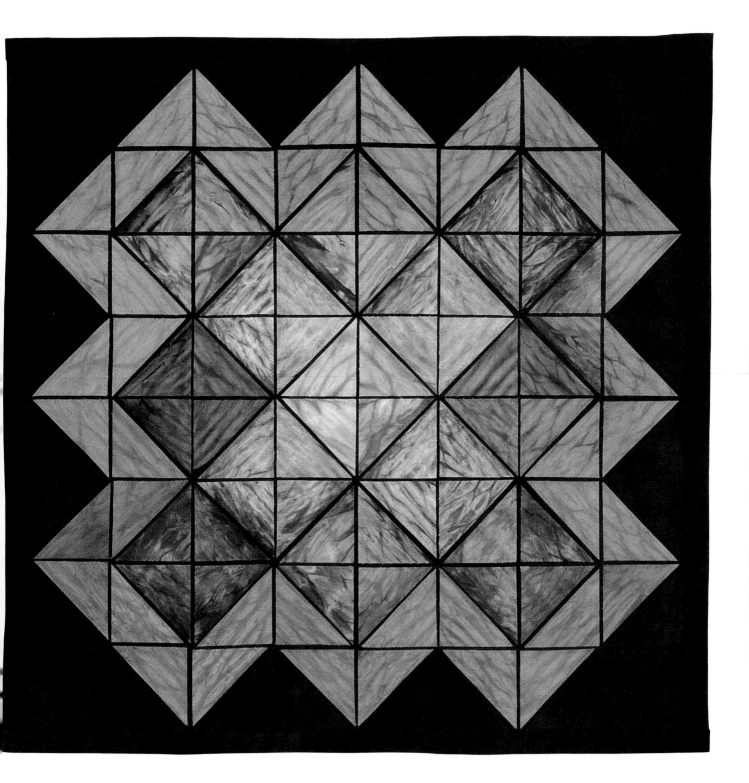

Carol Watkins
Boulder, Colorado
Passages I 40.5" x 34.5" 1999

Hand-dyed cottons, machine pieced, machine quilted.

I create one-of-a-kind fiber collages in two styles: abstract pieced art quilts incorporating my hand-dyed and painted fabric, and smaller works incorporating photographic imagery enhanced with many layers and colors of free motion machine embroidery.

Most recently I have been utilizing the computer, printer and my own photographs to digitally enhance images and print on cloth. I delight in combining new technology with the simplicity of thread and cloth. Recognizing the history of quiltmaking while incorporating new technologies excites me.

The *Passages* series of quilts incorporates hand-dyed fabric with large, bold, irregular shapes. It suggests passageways, the boundary delineating the point between here and there, the realized and the potential, the known and the mystery. This image continues to intrigue me.

Inspiration comes from almost anything, anywhere. I love the cracks in broken cement, fungi growing on a tree, rusted machinery and wildflowers. In 2003, I was an artist in residence at Rocky Mountain National Park, looking out on the Gore Range and contemplating the changes in my art and career. This led to a new way of seeing, attending to the fine details of a petal, the shape of a rock, the delicate pattern of lichen; a new way of working, creating heavily machine embroidered thread paintings. All of this is reflected in my art.

By education and profession I was a social worker, providing counseling to people for thirty years. I encouraged others to follow their dreams—could I do less? Therefore, in 2002 I left the work world to begin my new life as a full time artist. This was a leap of faith, but I recognized how much I needed to follow my heart. I love what I do and look forward to each day. My studio is place of solace and creativity. I am also a teacher with a desire to encourage aspiring art quilters to develop their own style.

Section Three

The New Century:
Confluence and Creation

Working...
Collect,
combine, define, compose,
discard, cover and peel.
Stop,
look, mark, cut,
refine, past and press.
Focus,
shift, touch, observe,
decide...
accept beauty

Joan Schulze, 1999

While art quiltmaking grew, hobby quilting grew even more during the early part of the new century. An estimated twenty million people were quilting, and whole textile and sewing equipment industries grew to support them. Robert Shaw, in his article on "unconventional quilts" in the November 2004 issue of *Quilters Newsletter Magazine*, estimated that quilters spent $2 billion annually on supplies alone. Not only were fabric manufacturers seeing increased business, quilt book publishers were riding the wave of expansion as well. Quilting embraced technology with the rush to digital imaging and printing, website development, Internet critique groups, and computerized sewing machines that do everything except cook dinner. And once again, thirty years after the landmark Holstein-van der Hoof exhibition, Abstract Design In American Quilts, the Whitney Museum of American Art punctuated its commitment to quilts as art with the powerful and eye-popping exhibition, The Quilts of Gee's Bend.

Still, out of these millions of people who thought of themselves as quilters, only a comparatively few are making art quilts. Quilt National continues, as does Visions, with higher and higher numbers of artists competing each year. Many of these artists are familiar names, such as Michael James, Nancy Erickson, Linda MacDonald, Terrie Hancock Mangat, M. Joan Lintault. The twenty or more years they have worked as studio artists continues to pay off with invitations to shows, museum placements, and highly visible public art projects such as Elizabeth Busch's Fort Lauderdale/Hollywood International (Florida) Airport project and Judith Trager's projects in public spaces in Denver, Colorado. Many of the newer, younger quilt artists are working hard to develop their individual styles, showing in local and regional exhibitions, and many are moving outside the quilt world to show their work in highly competitive shows like Crafts National and The Florida National.

The new century also began to disabuse the notion that African-American art quilts were somehow different than those made by suburban, white housewives. Art quilts began to reach a convergence of sorts. All styles of quilt art began to be recognized, from the minimalist color-field work of artists like Janet Steadman and Nancy Crow, to the folk art styles of Susan Shie and James Acord and Carolyn Mazloomi, to the experimental and digitally printed work of Patricia Mink and Miriam Nathan-Roberts.

And art quilts began to be seen in unlikely venues: hospitals, corporations and embassies. Their familiar yet new aspect makes them viewer-friendly and softens institutional settings. A new breed of knowledgeable collectors began to invest in art quilts, banking on their capital growth potential and enjoying their complexity.

The Rocky Mountain Quilt Museum has twenty-four art quilts from the early part of the twenty-first century. Among them are upcoming art quilters like Lisa Call, whose quilt *Structures #11* was on the 2003 Quilt National cover, and Molly Anderson, a Nebraska quilter whose use of unconventional materials makes her work interesting and complex.

The quilts from the first decade of the twenty-first century span all techniques and styles. Barbara D. Cohen, Diana Bunnell and Sandra Woock's works are created from fabric that has been "discharged," or had color removed using chlorine bleach techniques. Some of the pieces reflect traditional piecing and appliqué styles, such as Jan Magee's *Spears, Globes, Carpets and Climbers* and Elaine Spencer's *Every Vote Counts: Election 2000*. Some of the artists, like Arturo Alonzo Sandoval, Erika Carter, Virginia Harris, and Phil D. Jones, have used traditional academic composition to approach their work, whereas Betsy Cannon and Laura Wasilowski have used a free-form approach with fused fabrics, beads and puffy paint.

Two of the most exciting quilts from this decade are Michael James's *American Dream* and Gayle Fraas and Duncan Slade's *Watermark "D" Delta*. Both of these enigmatic quilts are printed using computer-aided digital technology to create the

images on the work. After the tops are printed and embellished, the quilts are then sandwiched and quilted in the traditional manner, just as quiltmakers have done throughout the ages.

Most important, the majority of the quilts from this decade are created by artists who have been, and still are, working the way artists always have — alone in their studios, exploring the images and ideas that create meaning in their art. Some of them, like Jean Ray Laury, have been at it for forty years. These artists have helped shape and change a powerful traditional medium, inspired other quilters to become artists and taught us to value changes that will become a new tradition.

American Dream *by Michael James*

Diana Bunnell
Boulder, Colorado
Black Minus Black Two   39" x 48"   2000

Discharged fabrics, acrylic paints, decorative threads, reverse appliqué, machine pieced, machine quilted.

The unpredictable and immediate results that can be achieved by discharging fabrics have always fascinated me. Various black fabrics discharge into white, tan, orange, even green patterns. Great variety can also be achieved by employing different methods to discharge the fabric. You can fold, stamp, dip, paint, etc., wherever your imagination takes you. I chose to combine my discharge experiments into a series of quilts titled *Black Minus Black* to illustrate the amazing versatility and spontaneity of this medium.

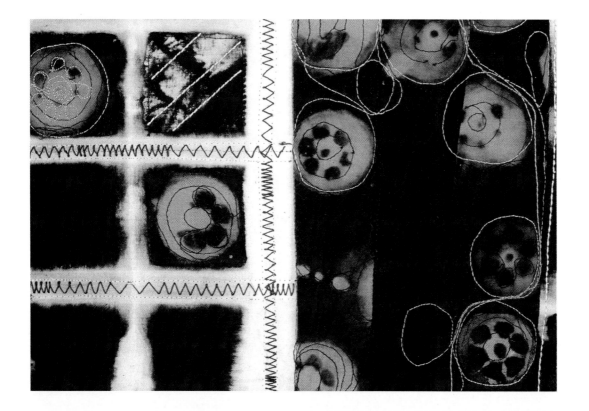

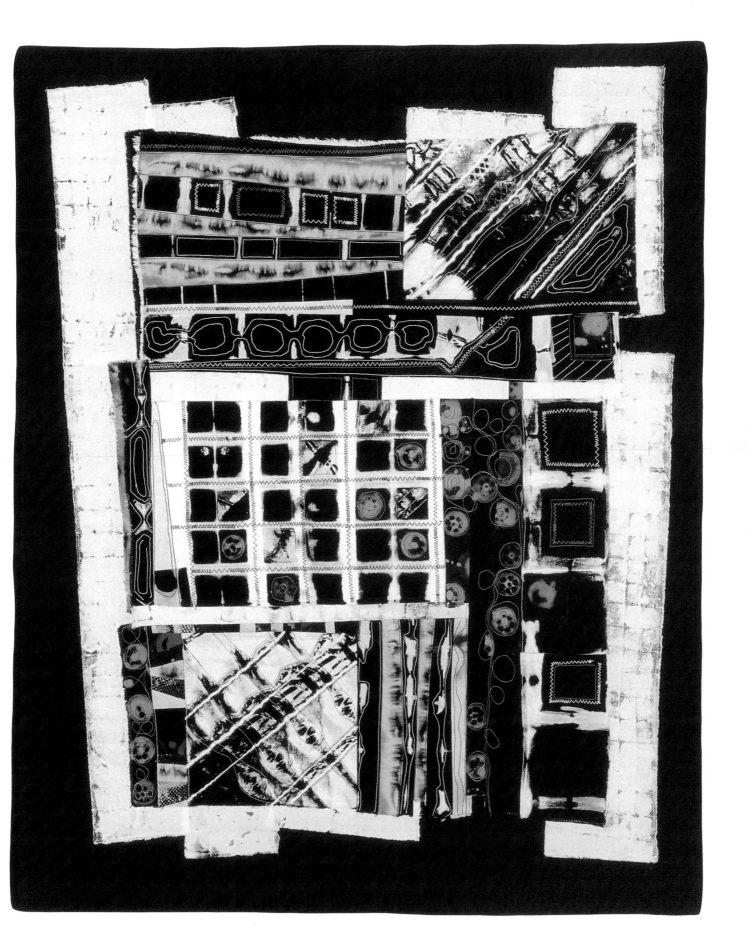

Virginia R. Harris
Santa Rosa, California
Seeing Red 40" x 54" 2000

Commercial fabrics, silks, cottons, synthetics, machine pieced, machine quilted.

The design of overlapping and interlocking circles baffled me for a long time. What colors to use? I tried a number of combinations and nothing worked. Then one morning the vision of a one-color quilt came to mind. Intriguing, but difficult, it seemed. Getting the diversity and impact I look for in my quilts using only one color presented a real challenge. The sixty-eight different red fabrics gave me the interest I was looking for in this design. Funny, one color can be so much more than that.

For years I searched for a creative outlet that engendered the passion of which artists speak. Photography had offered glimpses in the 1970s; writing did the same in the 1980s. In 1991 a friend asked a group of us each to make a quilt square for her fiftieth birthday. I checked six books out of the library and made a block. I made a second block because I didn't like the first one. The next day I bought fabric to make a quilt. As they say, the rest is history. I felt as if I had "come home." This experience changed how I relate in the world.

Through piecing together varied colors, shapes, fabrics, the variety and diversity of who I am becomes apparent. I explore the content and substance of the aspects of differentness through line, form, shape. Through quilting I push away the substitutions I have lived by and embrace my own personal aesthetic.

What does it look like to be fully in one's humanity? Quilt making and other fabric art offer me opportunities to search for the many answers, to use creating energy in constructive, life-giving ways, to use differences as the starting point to make a cohesive whole. The creative spirits in quilting allow me to create a new, truthful tradition from my personal aesthetic.

Carolyn L. Mazloomi
West Chester, Ohio
In the Winter of My Years, I Can Still See Springtime   44" x 48.5"   2000

Commercial fabrics, machine pieced, machine quilted.

"Much of my work deals with music. Quilts connect my spirit and soul to the music that has always been an element of my life. The words of a song, the emotion in a singer's voice, or the rhythm of music can inspire a new quilt. None of the quilts are planned, they just give birth to themselves. Quilts are my equivalent to making music; I never know the final result. Much like the jazz instrumentalist who improvises his music with such radically eloquent rhythms, quilts have vibes all their own. Quilts are visual soul food, and I hope the viewer can feel the spirit of the cloth."

Carolyn L. Mazloomi, artist, author, historian and curator, is acknowledged to be one of the most creative textile artists in the United States. She has produced an inspiring body of work, containing references to African-American life and history. Widely exhibited in the United States and internationally, her quilts have been included in five exhibitions at the Smithsonian's Renwick Gallery. Her artwork can be found in numerous important museums and corporate collections, such as the Wadsworth Museum, the Smithsonian Institution, American Museum of Design, Bell Telephone and Exxon. She has appeared on the *CBS Morning Show*, *Reading Rainbow*, *The Today Show*, CNN, and has been the subject of film documentaries. Mazloomi is one of six artists commissioned to create artwork for the National Underground Railroad Freedom Center Museum.

In 1985 she founded the Women of Color Quilters Network, an international organization with a membership of seventeen hundred, which has been a major force in fostering the work of African-American artists. Through Mazloomi's efforts WCQN members have had their quilts presented in prominent museums, galleries and international traveling exhibitions. She is a frequent consultant for

art exhibitions, authors, and historians.

In 1995, Mazloomi curated an art quilt exhibition in Beijing, China, as part of the United Nations Conference for Women, resulting in the book *Star Quilts* (Streelekha Press, Bangalore, India) which she coedited. She is also author of *Spirits of the Cloth*, given the "Best Non-Fiction Book of the Year" award by the American Library Association. Her latest book, *Threads of Faith*, was published in 2004 by the Museum of the American Bible Society. An exhibition based on this book will tour the United States for three years.

In 2003 Mazloomi was granted the first Ohio Heritage Fellowship Award deeming her to be one of the state's living cultural treasures. Fellows embody the highest level of artistic achievement in their work and the highest level of service in the teaching and service they do in their communities to ensure that their artistic traditions strengthen.

Mazloomi, a former aerospace engineer, has been involved in the economic development of women through the arts for over twenty years. Her organization, WCQN, has been recognized by the International Labour Department in Geneva and the United Nations for its developmental programs to help advance women.

Elaine Spencer
Fort Collins, Colorado
Every Vote Counts: Election 2000   25.5" x 35"   2000

Commercial fabrics, hand-screened cotton, machine pieced, machine quilted.

I make quilts for the sheer joy of it all. I like everything about quilting, from the flash of ideas and the research involved to the quest for the perfect fabrics to the final quilting stitches; everything, that is, except the ripping out! Much of my enjoyment of quilting comes from being with other quilters and sharing ideas, techniques and our lives.

I make traditional and contemporary quilts in cotton or wool, from king-size to small wall quilts, even potholders. I enjoy doing my own fabric dyeing and surface design. The traditional quilts provide a comforting structure during stressful times. Others are made to express my views about life events, and some are made to explore various techniques or for the pleasure of using special fabrics and colors.

I am a retired elementary school teacher who has been quilting for thirty-plus years. I live with my very supportive husband and two Great Danes who are therapy dogs. When I am not quilting, I am gardening, doing therapy dog work and enjoying my grown sons and their wives—and spoiling my five grandchildren.

My quilts have been shown widely, the most memorable being the Memories of Childhood international crib quilt contest sponsored by the Museum of American Folk Art in New York City, where my quilt about my brother seeing monsters in the basement was the grand-prize winner.

I started making quilts in Panama in the early 1970s. I had no idea what I was doing and had no tools—not even a ruler or proper fabric scissors—but that didn't deter me: I used dinner plates and boxes as templates. When we returned to the States, I took a quilt sampler class and went on from there. I learned to draft patterns, acquired the proper rulers and—wonder-of-wonders—a rotary cutter! I started out using traditional quilt patterns, and while I still use them, I also like to make quilts that fit the visions I see in my head—many more than I will ever have time to complete.

I cannot imagine my life without quilting.

1 18 35 52 69 86 104 121 138 156 173 190 208 225
2 19 36 53 70 87 105 122 139 157 174 191 209 226
3 20 37 54 71 88 106 123 140 158 175 192 210 227
4 21 38 55 72 89 107 124 141 159 176 193 211 228
5 22 39 56 73 90 108 125 142 160 177 194 212 229
6 23 40 57 74 91 109 126 143 161 178 195 213 230
7 24 41 58 75 92 110 127 144 162 179 196 214 231
8 25 42 59 76 93 111 128 145 163 180 197 215 232
9 26 43 60 77 94 112 129 146 164 181 198 216 234
10 27 44 61 78 95 113 130 147 165 182 199 217 235
11 28 45 62 79 96 114 131 148 166 183 200 218 236
12 29 46 63 80 97 115 132 149 167 184 201 219 237
13 30 47 64 81 98 116 133 150 168 185 202 220 238
14 31 48 65 82 99 117 134 151 169 186 203 221 239
15 32 49 66 83 100 118 135 152 170 187 204 222 240
16 33 50 67 84 101 119 136 153 171 188 205 223 241
17 34 51 68 85 102 120 137 154 172 189 206 224 242
103 155 207

J. Bruce Wilcox
Denver, Colorado
Brushstroke 62" x 62" 2000

Commercial fabrics, machine pieced, hand quilted in cotton crochet cord.

I have recently more fully recognized my Art Path as my Spiritual Practice.

Listening to music most of the time…Designing, both the sketching and envisioning parts…Drawing and constructing the cardboard patterns…Pulling together the myriad, often unrelated textiles…Cutting out the always more than I need group of fabrics, or my dismemberment process…Laying out the mass of print and pattern and color until it gels, thereby ordering chaos…Machine constructing, or remembering the various component parts…Setting up to quilt the never before existing, yet reborn single-pieced surface…Hand quilting, always in a very high state of meditation…And then finishing and signing the new work, freeing it from me in a completion exercise…

I recognized that following my childhood interests would be following my right destiny. I recognized that working in my fiber medium would balance my masculine and feminine energies, allowing a state of wholeness to manifest. I recognized that in giving it all up to my Art, I surrendered to the Creative Spirit of the Universe. In doing so I recognized the Oneness of all things. Including me.

At the age of eight I learned to sew. Fabric and pattern-work interested me, and I taught myself how to create soft-sculpture figures, puppets, art embroidery and knotting. I took drawing and painting classes, but my love of the tactile prevailed. My first one-man show was at the age of sixteen. Fascinated by Alexander Calder, I designed and built mobiles and was invited to hang a series at the Weber County Library in Ogden, Utah. After graduating from Roy High School I attended the University of Utah.

Since 1977 my work has hung in nearly one hundred exhibits and have been published

in books, magazines and catalogs. After my initial artistic success, I shifted away from pieced work. I began doing line drawings transferred to a single piece of fabric that were hand-quilted using heavy cord, a 2" needle and my trademark backstitch. I then stretched, painted and framed them. I began showing this work in 1981. In 1990 I returned to pieced work, because an art quilt group had recently formed in Colorado. I began to show extensively in Colorado, and in 1993 I hung a two-man show in Salt Lake City.

I've always followed my own artistic path, and I've never taken classes from any art quilt teachers. My work is not influenced by others in the movement. I believe that because I created my first art quilt in 1977, my work has always been on the leading edge of this movement. I never thought of my work as anything but art, and even the functional pieces I've created in twenty-seven years are still art first. In 2002 I finished my first stretched painted piece in many years, which showed in SAQA's Challenging Tradition. My true focus has never shifted. I'm an artist, not a quilt maker. I've never considered myself a quilt maker, and I never will. I create because nothing less makes sense.

Charlotte Ziebarth
Boulder, Colorado
Sea Skins Diptych
24" x 40.5" each   2000

My work blends fabrics and quilting
with photographs, digital design and
a love of nature.

The inspiration for most of my work comes
from the forms, colors and patterns of the
natural world—leaves, trees, clouds, rocks.
I take many photographs when I hike
around my region and when I travel. I use
these photos as the basis for my digital
painting. My camera is the starting point in
portraying some of the pleasures and mysteries
of everyday life. It records things others might not always notice. It provides the basic images for my digital
explorations. Printing these images on cloth juxtaposes the old and the new. I like the art quilt medium because
of the stitched repetition of line, the patterning of block arrangements and grids, and the sculpted bas-relief
effects of layered cloth and stitching.

Beginning with white fabric, I then dye it using various methods of resist and silkscreen. I sometimes also paint
fabric using textile paints and inks applied with stamps, stencils, sponges and brushes. I then print directly on
specially treated fabrics with my inkjet printer the digital designs that I have derived from my original photos.

All of these "designed by me" fabrics are combined in a collage-like way to create my fused-appliqué surfaces. These are embellished and quilted with freemotion machine stitching technique. Sewing is the last layer of imagery applied to the piece. It creates the thread-drawn lines and the bas-relief effect.

Born in Chicago and raised in the Midwest, my family and I have lived in Boulder, Colorado, for more than thirty years. My husband, Ken, is a manager for Boulder County, and we have a daughter who is a math professor at Earlham College in Indiana. Although I have a background in psychology, I have worked with cloth all my life as a weaver, clothing designer, knitter and quilter. Widely exhibited and collected, my work is known for my rich color usage, both in my handwoven tapestries and in art quilt/collage techniques. When not working in the studio I can be found hiking in the mountains, walking in Boulder, attending concerts, listening to opera, reading, or making mosaics from broken pottery. In the summer of 2003 I had the incredible opportunity to be an artist in residence in Rocky Mountain National Park, where I took zillions of pictures and enjoyed watching both the elk and the tourists.

Molly Anderson
Minden, Nebraska
Nosegay 29" x 30" 2001

Cotton batiks, embroidery, ribbonwork, beading, hand pieced, hand appliquéd.

My grandmother Luella, who is an accomplished "traditional" quilter, and my mother, Nancy Tomsen, taught me the basics of quilting. I would describe myself as an avid quilter with an art background. The watercolor-hexagon quilts combine both of these interests and allow endless possibilities. They are both quilts that happen to be art pieces and art pieces that happen to be quilts. The watercolor-hexagon quilts came about quite by accident. I became bored following patterns, so I began doing original designs in watercolor quilting. At the same time, I was paper-piecing a traditional grandmother's flower garden quilt with 1940s reproduction fabrics. The squares and rectangles used in traditional watercolor quilting did not give me the blends I wanted, so I tried the hexagon shapes I had used in the grandmother's flower garden. The rounded shape of the hexagon seemed to be the trick for the watercolor blends that I was looking for. In 1977, I completed my first piece, *Summer Landscape*, using this technique. With the completion of each piece, I learn things that can make the following quilt better, artistically and technically. They seem to continually evolve.

I graduated from Bethany College in Lindsborg, Kansas, with a degree in secondary and elementary art education. I create, exhibit and lecture on my contemporary textiles and fabric application on fiberglass.

Laura Cater-Woods
Billings, Montana
Canyon Music: March   36" x 44"   2001

Cotton batiks, hand-dyed and painted fabrics, machine appliquéd, machine quilted.

"The work begins with line and pattern found in driftwood, shell, rock, bits and pieces from the gardens. Marks left by time and natural process fascinate me. The power of wind and water to shape and form the landscape is compelling. I am obsessed with the idea that time in its abstract sense is reflected in such a concrete object as a shell or as ephemeral a form as a leaf. Working with manipulated and altered fabric and the stitched surface offers a process of marking that is interactive and that adds layers of associations to the imagery. The forms take on new meanings as they are developed in cloth. Meanings change again as viewers bring their experience to the process."

Laura is a full time studio artist with an extensive exhibition record and awards. Her work is held in numerous public and private collections. After completing an MFA in Painting she began to integrate her love of fabric and thread with her approach to drawing and painting. Her images explore the textures and rhythms of details from the landscape, often interwoven with eccentric grids.

She has completed commissions for Public Art and Percent for Art Projects, including Montana State Hospital at Warm Springs and the *HORSE of course!* project in Billings and recently completed a site-specific mural for the Montana Development Center.

In addition to commissions, exhibitions and presenting workshops across the country, Laura curates traveling exhibits of small format fiber art. She juried Textile Medium V, was Co-Director of Fine Focus '02, juror for Quilt 21, American Art Quilts 2002 and Co-Curator for Materials and Meaning, Mixed Bag Gallery, Houston. Her current project is Dreaming the Garden. In 1988-89 she was honored with a Montana Arts Council Fellowship in Visual Arts, Mixed Media.

Marilyn Chaffee
Poway, California
Skyworks #4   12" x 8"   2001

Cottons, acrylic-painted raw-edge appliqué, foiling, machine and hand quilting, hand embellishment.

My early work centered around traditional patchwork and large wall quilts, but my more recent pieces have used more experimental techniques and a smaller format. This diminutive scale offers opportunities to explore surface design, fabric collage techniques, expressive stitching and more informal compositions.

Over the years my work has appeared in *Fiberarts* magazine, Quilt National, *Quilting Arts* magazine and on the cover of *Quilter's Newsletter Magazine*. It has been acquired by both public and private collectors, is currently part of the Fine Focus '04 traveling exhibition and was recently published in the new book *Design! A Lively Guide to Design Basics* (Lark Books, 2004).

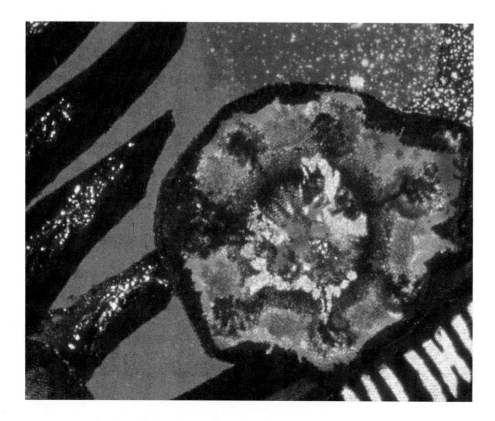

Jean Ray Laury
Clovis, California
Girls of the Golden West 31.5" x 36.5" 2001

Hand silkscreened and painted fabrics, machine pieced, machine quilted.

"This piece was based on my idea of the cowgirl as the epitome of the Independent Woman. I envisioned her running a ranch, riding, being a rugged individual, facing the elements. Then I realized she was now wearing Calvin Klein jeans and had her own website and dot-com address. She had moved past my concept, but I still see her as a very colorful character.

"*Girls of the Golden West* is my original design from a drawing. I made a photo silk screen of the drawing and printed it onto the white or light fabrics. I then used an assortment of screens and stencils to print all the pattern work—polka dots, stripes, patterns, are all hand-printed. I also printed the stripes for the sashing.

"For the lettering, I use a computer, making a print out of the selected words. I make Thermofax stencils and then screen print the words onto the cloth. There are also areas that are hand-painted and hand-drawn with permanent marker. The work is accomplished using heat-set water-base paints.

"I love to draw and screen print, and this includes both. There is almost always an underlying structure in my work that relates to traditional quilts."

Jean Ray Laury is a freelance artist and writer with one-woman and group shows at museums, galleries and universities across the country. Her quilts are in both private and museum collections. Quilting, writing, folk arts and crafts are among her many interests, as are reading, cooking (eating!) and hiking. Jean and her husband, Frank (retired from California State University, Fresno) live in the foothills, where they are visited by wild turkeys, deer, foxes, family and friends.

Jean's teaching and lecturing have taken her worldwide—from Japan and Australia to Belgium, France, Norway, Austria and South Africa.

The overwhelming success of Jean Ray Laury's lectures and teaching rests in part on her willingness to share her innovative approaches, her tremendous energies and her dynamic visual statements. Insight, wisdom and humor grow out of a professional commitment coupled with an awareness of human needs and family values. The enthusiastic response from audiences of all ages, and from men as well as women, attests to her ability to touch a vital spot in the creative make up of us all.

Ed Johnetta Miller
Hartford, Connecticut
Reawakening the Spirit II   60" x 48"   2001

Commercial cottons, silks, African prints, machine pieced, machine quilted.

A fiber artist, quilter, teacher, curator and lecturer, Ed Johnetta Miller is acknowledged to be one of the most creative and colorful improvisational quiltmakers in the United States. Widely exhibited at home and internationally, her quilts can be found in numerous important museums such as The National Gallery of the Smithsonian Institution, Nelson Mandela's National Museum, Capetown, South Africa, the Wadsworth Atheneum Museum of Art, Hartford, Connecticut, and the Rocky Mountain Quilt Museum, as well as in corporate and private collections. The Sunday *New York Times* featured Ed Johnetta in the "Best of the Best" series in 2002. She has received the most prestigious artistic award for the State of Connecticut, the Governor's Award in 2003, the Amistad Foundation's First Presidents award, 2003, the Leadership of Greater Hartford's Arts and Cultural Award, 2003. In 2004 she received the Vision Award for Arts and Culture from the Charter Oak Cultural Center.

Ed Johnetta has been featured on HGTV's *The Modern Masters*, Debbie Allen's series, *Cool Women*, public television, Tokyo, Japan, and her woven creations were worn by Phylicia Rashad on *The Cosby Show*. *Quilting Quarterly* magazine featured Ed Johnetta in summer 2004.

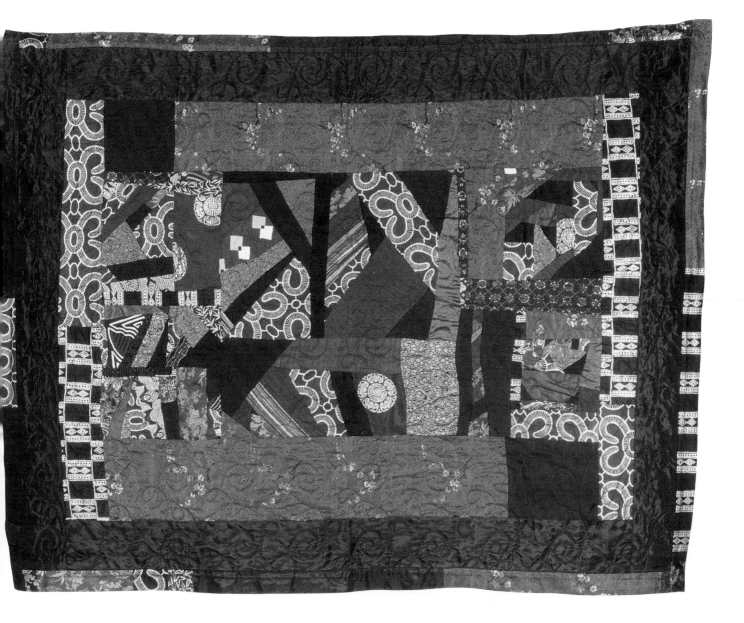

Judith Tomlinson Trager
Boulder, Colorado
Bosque Sunrise 28" x 40"   2001

Hand-dyed cottons, commercial fabrics, silk organza, handmade stamped images in gold acrylic, machine pieced (raw-edge appliqué), machine quilted.

I grew up with quilts. My earliest memories are of sitting under the quilting frame in a bright room looking up at the patterns overhead while my mother and her six sisters quilted. The rhythm of their stitches and the warmth of their voices as they gossiped filled me with happiness. My first quilt was made when I was about eight as a church project; I've never stopped, and more than fifty years and more than three hundred quilts have passed.

Quilts have been the threads that bound our family together. They were everywhere: on beds, chairs, sofas and sometimes on walls. They still are. Kids carried them around. Dolls and teddy bears were wrapped in them. Even the dog had one. Fabric was a necessity in every month's budget.

I moved from traditional quiltmaking to art quilts after studying painting at the University of Minnesota as an undergraduate. Suddenly my quilts became a canvas on which to paint, do surface design, stitching and collage—and anything else that seemed appropriate: buttons, beads, shiny paper, silk appliqués.

Quilting became my career beginning with teaching a class at the Stanford University YMCA in 1979. For many years I fit my art and teaching around "real" jobs—university

administrator, teddy bear salesman, home renovator. In 1989, with both children in university, we moved Boulder, Colorado where my husband joined the faculty. I retired to the studio.

My quilts are now in collections around the world, including several United States embassies, many hospitals, public buildings and corporate headquarters. In 1995, I received a CO-Visions Award from the Colorado Arts Council and the NEA. That same year, I had my first quilt juried into Quilt National. In 1992 I began curating museum exhibitions and currently have two exhibitions traveling nationally: Potluck and Elements from the Front Range Contemporary Quilters. I continue to work on public-art projects, most recently a three-piece installation at Red Rocks Museum and Amphitheatre in Colorado, and this year I am the artist representative on the program evaluation panel for public art for the city of Denver. My work has been widely published, including in *Fiberarts Design Books V* and *VI*, *The Colorado Quilt*, and many others. I have appeared on HGTV's *Simply Quilts* as well. I have taught in Europe, Australia, New Zealand and the United States and currently accept students for weeklong residency programs at my Boulder studio.

Arturo Alonzo Sandoval
Lexington, Kentucky
Accidentally on Purpose 30.5" x 46.5" 2001

Digitized image on canvas, acrylics, netting, variegated and monofilament threads, Mylar, polyester edging and braid, machine appliquéd and quilted.

As an artist my philosophy is work produces results. Beauty is found in nature and in the objects that humankind has created here in this physical space. It is from nature that humankind obtains inspiration, materials, ideas and designs that permeate our world. Currently, recent explorations of space with satellites and the Hubble and Chandra telescopes have provided new information about the universe, stars and planets. Scientists and engineers have taken this new information to heart and have predicted that human beings will inhabit other worlds. My Millennium series creations in silk and mixed media express this new knowledge of current scientific discovery and carry my message of HOPE for humankind.

In searching for content in the vein of my planetary work among the list of oxymorons presented to the artists for the exhibition Oxymorons: Absurdly Logical Quilts my first choice was divinely appointed with the selection of *Accidentally on Purpose*. In taking great liberty with design and content I am depicting the universe not as black and empty, but filled with intense energy, color, light, pattern and texture. The viewpoint of the spectator for this new work is that of the observer.

My process starts with discoveries from my pile of recycled student-painted canvases from years of collecting. Working in a direct appliqué method I use circular pieces to dominate the compositions. These ideas are designed to relate to the Biblical statement, "My father's house has many mansions." I then develop atmospheric and spatial elements for the background areas using transparent fabrics and machine embroidery. The use of the reflective Mylar grid as a design element symbolizes my vision of the eternal quality of time. The pieces are then backed with cotton fabrics adhered using polymer medium. Edges are finished off using machine stitching, and for this work I sew hanging and weight sleeves to the backing.

115

Sandra Woock
Bethesda, Maryland
Eclipse   32" x 60"   2001

Hand-discharged fabrics, machine pieced, machine quilted.

In this piece I incorporated surface design techniques to create an abstract image playing with circles, patterns and positive/negative space. The free-motion machine stitching allows me the freedom to paint with thread and add the lines that echoes through the piece.

I selected *Eclipse* as my contribution to this collection as it is a significant example of my studio work. I work each piece as a complete thought, a tangible journey influenced by events in my life. My fiber art is pronounced by my strong emphasis on surface design utilizing resist and discharge techniques, which I have used since 1996. In this case, I have pinned, clamped, tied, wrapped and painted to block areas from the subtracting nature of the bleaching action to create my abstract imagery. Without adding an over-dye process, I was satisfied with the earthy tones and coloring of the commercially dyed black fabric.

While I composed the series of circles through the middle, the union of the two halves became more obscure and hidden, developing opposing personality as individual columns of positive/negative patterns reflecting each other. The silent velocity of the circles prompted a working title that stuck.

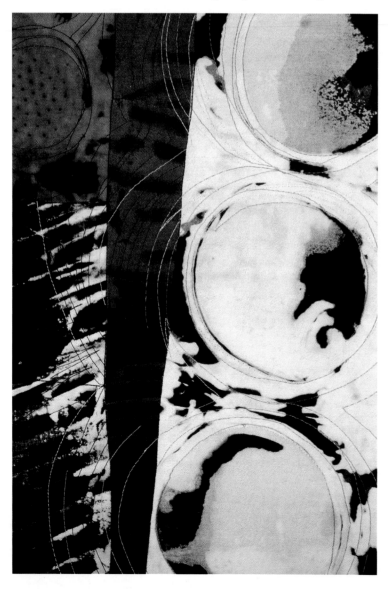

The top was then layered with batting and backing fabric. Free motion machine quilting allows me to add the element of drawing to complete my art work with the intimate expression and tactile quality that I could not achieve with another medium.

Where were you when...?
After 9/11 2001, everyone knows this question refers to that moment, that day, that space in time, that tragedy. On 9/11 I was chasing a deadline sewing *Eclipse*, expecting smooth creative flow to the finish. As I trudged through that emotional week, every task seemed a memorial to those whose numbers were being counted. This piece was still about hiding, obscuring light and separation: two columns, looming, stretched out under the arm of my sewing machine. The victims who had fallen and their families—even though it didn't start out that way, it did become about them.

Yes, the country did change with that event. Unchanging is our inability to predict what tomorrow will bring or how long we will be able to continue what we are presently doing. To do the best today and continue to pass on history and knowledge to others always is our lesson to remember.

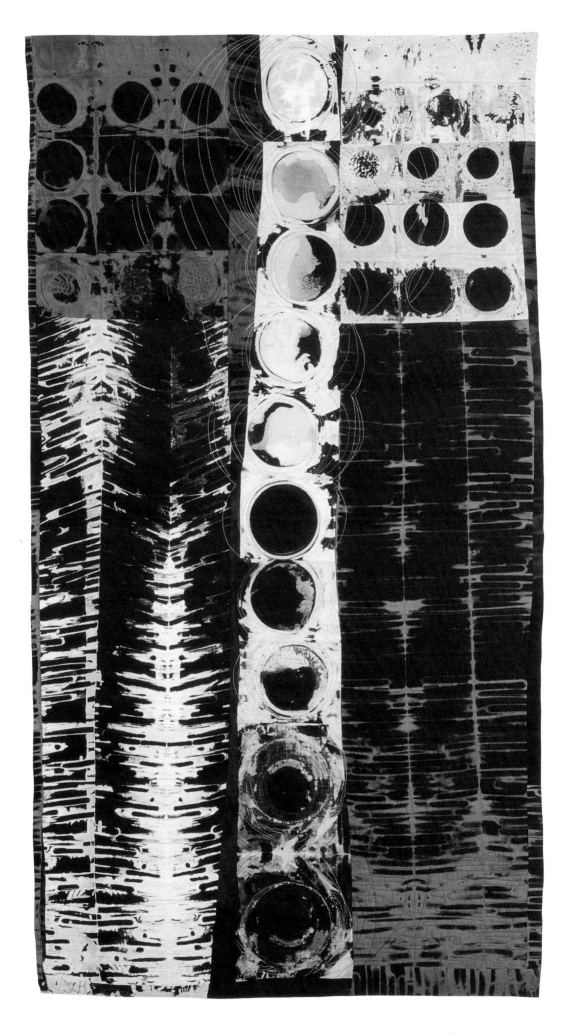

Lisa Call
Parker, Colorado
Structures #5   39" x 67"   2002

Hand-dyed fabrics, machine pieced, machine quilted.

I have been making quilts for twenty-five years, beginning in high school. Intially, pieced traditional bed quilts were my focus, although they had a contemporary look with bright, bold colors and original block designs or settings. During this time I completed a BA and an MA in computer science and worked as a software engineer at one of the nation's top computer science research labs, with quilt making as a casual hobby, making only a few quilts a year.

In 1992, I left the workforce to stay home with my children and looked to replace the intellectual challenge of a highly technical career with quilting. Within a year I turned to more original work as it was more stimulating and rewarding. Over the next several years I struggled to find my artistic voice. I took workshops with several well-known quilters and played with many of the new techniques being used, yet I was never satisfied with the results of these experiments as they didn't meet my creative needs.

It wasn't until I took an intensive seven-day workshop with Nancy Crow in 1999 that I found a methodology that was right for me. With improvisational piecing techniques I am able to refine my design throughout the entire construction process, each seam sewn and each shape cut requires me to consider the proportions and design of the entire composition. I have continued to study with Nancy almost every year, always looking to refine and improve my artistic skills. While these construction techniques are rooted in tradition the resulting quilts are vivid geometric abstract contemporary artwork.

I work in series with a motif unifying the separate works within a collection. This element is more recognizable in some work than others as the size, shape and composition evolves over time. Color is of primary importance and is combined, intuitively, in unexpected ways, employing a unique palette of cotton fabrics I hand-dye. It can take weeks or months to make a single quilt, as the individual elements in the composition are freehand cut, one at a time, without a pattern. They are then placed onto a flannel-covered studio wall, where I improvise, planning as I construct. The design continues to mature as the pieces are manipulated so they can be sewn together. Extensive machine stitching adds rich texture to the work by echoing the shapes underneath or by creating a complementary secondary pattern on the surface.

Much of my work evokes my interpretation of the colors and landscape of the American southwest, where I spend considerable time backpacking in the Grand Canyon, hiking to the top of Colorado's splendid Fourteeners, photographing canyon walls in New Mexico or running marathons on back roads and trails.

Laura Wasilowski
Elgin, Illinois
Surf's Up   40" x 31"   2002

Hand-dyed cottons, fused, machine quilted.

I've always been an artist. Creating is what I do.

As a child I learned to sew through the 4-H program and later used those skills as a costume design major in college. Part of my degree program was learning to dye fabric. My first art business began in the 1980s. I hand-dyed, stamped, silk-screened and painted fabrics that I converted into clothing to sell in boutiques.

A new neighbor, Janet Dye, introduced me to quiltmaking. Together we attended a program given by Caryl Bryer Fallert at a local quilt guild. It was after seeing Caryl's beautiful work that I made the link between using my own hand-dyed fabrics to create this new medium called art quilts.

Soon after, another new friend, Melody Johnson, introduced me to the technique of "fusing" which has become the construction method I use for all my quilts. Fusing is using a dry glue (fusible web) on the back of fabrics that is activated by the heat of an iron. I soon discovered that fusing was the most direct route from a design idea in my head to the realization of that idea. It gave me the freedom to create any image I wanted, allowing my work to be looser and more inventive.

The art quilts I make often document my life. They tell stories of my family, friends and home. Some relate events in my family's history like the story of my mother's

kitchen on baking day. Other quilts picture everyday objects found in our home like chairs, irons and teapots. Each object becomes a beloved cartoon character with a personality and life all its own.

My life has changed a great deal since that first 4-H sewing class. Now I create art quilts and teach and lecture about contemporary quilt making. I own Artfabrik, makers of hand-dyed fabric and threads, and am author of *Fusing Fun: Fast Fearless Art Quilts*.

One thing I have retained from my early years is my sense of whimsy. When I make a new quilt I feel the delight of a child cutting out red construction paper. It is a feeling of freedom, joy, happiness.

I am very fortunate to be an art quilter.

Barbara D. Cohen
Denver, Colorado
Urban Voice   48" x 42"   2003

Hand-dyed cottons, discharged cottons, commercial fabrics, raw-edge appliqué, cotton, rayon and metallic threads, machine pieced, machine quilted.

Barbara D. Cohen has always been an artist, and her life revolves around the arts. Raised in New York City, she first studied painting at the Art Student's League of New York as a teenager. She eventually attended the Carnegie-Mellon Institute in Pittsburgh, Pennsylvania as a painting and design student. As a graphics major she earned a BA at Parsons School of Design and New York University.

Cohen began her career working for George Tcherny, noted graphic designer. Later she worked for eleven years at Dell Publishing as a book designer, including eight years as the art director for the hardbound and paperback adult, juvenile and textbook divisions. In 1976, Cohen and her family moved to Denver, where she pursued her personal artistic talents including hand-painting and marketing one-of-a kind clothing. She rediscovered the joy of using her hands to make things that she loved doing as a child.

Her involvement in fiber art began with an invitation to take a quiltmaking workshop with Nancy Crow in 1991 that introduced her to designing and making contemporary art quilts. Struggling at first with the sewing machine, Cohen moved easily into designing and creating with fabric. Her work continues to evolve as she makes collage paintings in cloth with stitching. Often abstract, the work is always evocative of personal events and emotions. She creates hand-dyed fabrics that show strong patterning coming from her graphic-design background. Cohen works intuitively, always striving to create bold shapes that will catch the viewer's eye from a distance and entice him or her in for a closer look. She uses paint, embroidery and appliqué in a contemporary way in order to create details. Cohen is thankful to those fiber artists who have proceeded her in the art quilt movement so that traditional methods of hand-piecing, quilting and making "all the points meet" are no longer required in this art form.

Cohen's work has been exhibited nationally and has been juried into major shows including Quilt National and Fiberarts International. She has been included in the *Fiberarts Design Book Seven* and her art quilt, *Benediction* appears on the cover of the book *The Mitzvah of Healing*. Cohen also creates custom one-of-a-kind Judaic ritual objects such as Sabbath challah covers and Passover matzoh covers.

In keeping with her appreciation of various art forms, Cohen has recently begun to produce mosaic objects and custom furniture using the ancient technique of piqué assiette, which involves breaking up ceramic tiles, dishes and ornamental objects and recycling them into new pieces of fine decorative art. She believes that mosaics are a natural outgrowth of piecing art quilts.

Gayle Fraas and Duncan Slade
Edgecomb, Maine
Watermark "D" Delta   57" x 57"   2003

Whole-cloth, painted, screen-printed, digitally printed cotton, with reactive dyes. Machine quilted.

We have never made a traditional quilt, nor have we ever held a full-time job. As undergraduates in 1974 we combined our interests in screen-printed fabric and made a quilt.

By the late 1970s our work focused on man's relationship with the natural world, framing literal (sometimes idealized) views with pattern and border designs, forming the genesis of the conceptual center of all our work. For us "it is the specifics of a site that meaning and perceptions are engendered.

"Places are stories told through the remnants of history and experiences of residents, through the luxury of wealth, the struggle for existence and the endurance of nature."

Our quilts are whole-cloth quilts (the top surface being one piece of fabric). Each work is painted and in some cases screen-printed, and for several years now we have included some digital printing, all with fiber-reactive dyes on cotton broadcloth. Printing allows us to expedite some of our pattern work. At times we further refine printing with overpainting and shading. Landscapes are painted to balance with ornamental elements. We have always preferred these dyes as they are extremely versatile on cellulose fiber, for their transparency and for the fact that they don't alter the hand of the fabric.

On occasion we will teach a workshop sharing our knowledge of the dyes with other quilt-makers and textile artists, many of whom have gone on to exhibit work, publish and teach, each adapting and expanding dye painting, making it an integral component of the current quiltmaking vocabulary.

Our work pieces together the tools and materials of folk art, applied art and fine art. Works are informed by other textiles, medieval manuscript illumination, pop art, the Hudson River School painters and the graphic language of flags.

Our visual conversation has continued for thirty years. We both draw and paint and, regardless of who executes a specific piece, all is signed with both last names in respect for the aesthetic involvement we share. Each piece is considered part of a single body of work.

Wendy Hill
Sun River, Oregon
Falling Into Liquid 41.5" x 41.5" 2003

Cotton batiks, machine pieced, machine quilted with rayon, metallic and monofilament threads.

Listening to public radio one day, I heard a story about surfing and the feeling of stepping into the wave. This provoked thoughts about what it would be like to fall into water, to blend with water, to see the world from inside water. I wondered how I could evoke a strong feeling of water. The result is this quilt, *Falling Into Liquid.*

My first memories are of the colors around me. My parents supported my drive to create from the beginning. I started drawing and coloring as soon as I could sit up and hold a crayon. My father often sat with me while I drew pictures. Despite my young age, his advice made sense: don't just draw a tree with a trunk and branches, give each tree character so each one will be different. A couple of years later I was frustrated with my drawing of a clock with too many numbers. He told me anyone could copy a clock, but it took a special person to draw one like mine. I believed him and in turn started to develop a belief in myself as well.

As I became a little older, I played with craft supplies and fabric scraps. I made a doll quilt with my mother's help and started sewing on my own. In high school I explored a variety of media, including such things as acrylic paintings, burlap boots, pencil renderings, a vinyl bikini bathing suit, oil paintings and a raincoat made out of bread wrappers. I began college studying art but became a teacher instead. There is an art to teaching, as anyone knows who has been held captive by a teacher with no creative spirit.

I continued to follow my ideas both in the classroom and with a variety of media. My first quilt, a king size replica of the floor of the Taj Majal, was made with no-wale corduroy. Color and texture have always been at the heart of everything in my life, from gardening to textiles to engaging high school students. Always dabbling in a variety of projects, my bed quilts hung on the wall until they were needed for warmth, while I took out the art supplies to create "art." One day my worlds of art, teaching and quilting collided. From then on I saw the cross connections of all of my interests.

Everything is a kind of composition if looked at a certain way.

All visual arts, including quilts, share common aesthetic concerns. With art quilts, form takes precedence over function, but quilts-as-blankets are also a kind of canvas. If there is a line between art and craft, it is a difference built out of debate, not something tangible. The important thing is to do the work, just keep doing the work and let the perspective that comes with reflection and the passage of time make sense of it all.

Michael James
Lincoln, Nebraska
American Dream 67" x 44"   2003

Digitally developed and printed images on cottons with reactive dyes, machine pieced, machine quilted.

"My interest in color and its interplay with visual movements and with illusory space have been consistent concerns throughout my development as a quiltmaker. While the work has taken various forms over the years and has responded in various ways to different techniques and materials, those formal concerns have governed my studio activities."

Although the pieced and quilted fabric constructions of Michael James are strongly rooted in the tradition of American quiltmaking they nonetheless reflect an idiosyncratic approach to this centuries-old art form. Michael's approach to quiltmaking is influenced as much by his training as a painter as by his study of the history of American quiltmaking. This is reflected in the artist's first two books, *The Quiltmaker's Handbook* and *The Second Quiltmaker's Handbook,* making them classic guidebooks for the novice quiltmaker. With bachelor and master of fine art degrees in painting (University of Massachusetts-Dartmouth, 1971, which also awarded him an honorary doctor of fine arts degree in 1992, and Rochester Institute of Technology, Rochester, New York, 1973), he is among a group of formally trained artists who turned in the 1970s from mainstream media to the tactile and sensual appeal that quilts offer.

Michael has twice been the recipient of Visual Artists' Fellowships from the National Endowment for the Arts and of Craftsmens' Fellowships from the Artists' Foundation, Boston. In 1990 he lived and worked at La Napoule Art Foundation on a United States/ France Exchange NEA Fellowship. In 1992 he was inducted into the Quilter's Hall of Fame. In 1994, he was honored with the first biannual Society of Arts and Crafts Award in Boston.

Michael was one of five American textile artists invited to participate in the eighth International Trienniale of Tapestry in 1995 in Lodz, Poland. He exhibits his work widely internationally and was honored with a twenty-five-year retrospective at the Museum of the American Quilter's Society. His work has been in six Quilt Nationals as well as in invitational shows at the Museum of Art and Design in New York City. In 2001 he was named a fellow of the American Craft Council. He is a 2003 recipient of a Lincoln (Nebraska) Arts Council Mayor's Arts Award for Artistic Achievement.

Michael's studio is located in Lincoln, Nebraska, where he is Ardis James Professor of the College of Education and Human Sciences at the University of Nebraska-Lincoln. There he teaches courses in textile design and also serves as a faculty fellow of the International Quilt Study Center. In addition, Michael lectures and leads workshops on color and design in America, Europe and Japan.

Phil D. Jones
Denver, Colorado
Red Rover 28" x 33" 2003

Hand-dyed cotton roving, silk roving and papers, wool roving, machine quilted with rayon, metallic and monofilament threads.

It is my intent that the Garden of Life series of work provides the viewer images with a contemplative or meditative quality. This series is about seeing nature as metaphor; about birth, life, growth, death, change. It's about irony, dichotomy, double or reverse meanings and conceptual twists. Koans.

While portraying landscape scenes, this series is about relationships and process. *Red Rover* reminds me of the many stances and games groups of people play at various gatherings. *Red Rove*r utilizes hand-dyed fabrics, handmade silk paper and other felted fibers, highly machine stitched to obtain this vision.

Betsy Cannon
Centennial, Colorado
Shrine to the Prairie Chicken   28" x 35"   2004

Commercial cottons, synthetics, embellished with rick-rack trim, beads, sequins, silver lamé stars, machine appliquéd, machine quilted.

Betsy Cannon is a contemporary quiltmaker whose work has been shown nationally and internationally. Her quilts are full of bright colors and embellishment and have whimsical themes—cactus and chicken legs are recent features. "I think that we spend too much time on the negative and need to focus on the silly things in life. It's my mission."

Betsy owes her love of most tacky things to her west-Texas upbringing. That, along with having a wonderful grandmother who taught her to sew and had her making little stitched pieces in the late '60s. Over time, those pieces started to become more quilt-like and then started to acquire embellishment. "I think that puffy paint is one of the best things to happen to fabric in a long time", she says. "It gives a piece great surface texture, color, and is such fun to apply!" During trips to China, Betsy collected sequins and beads that have become a part of her quilts as well. She loves the sparkle and excess that they give her pieces. "Excess is never enough—it's something to live by!"

Erika Carter
Belleview, Washington
Solitude IX   40" x 32.5"   2004

Discharged cotton, silk organza, acrylic paints, machine appliqué, hand embroidery, machine pieced, machine quilted.

Erika Carter is an award-winning art quilter whose evocative wall quilts have been exhibited throughout the United States, Sweden and Japan. Her quilts have been seen in numerous Quilt Nationals. Among her many honors and awards are an Award of Merit at the 1995 Quilt National and a 1991 and 2001 Artist Trust grant. She is the author of an acclaimed book about her art, *Erika Carter: Personal Imagery in Art Quilts* (Fiber Studio Press, 1996), and her work has been reproduced and written about in numerous books and magazines including *Art Quilt Magazine, American Craft* and *Surface Design Journal*. Her work is also included in many collections, including those of the Museum of Art and Design in New York and the Museum of American Quilter's Society in Paducah, Kentucky. Carter lives and works in Bellevue, Washington.

Jan Magee
Denver, Colorado
Spears, Globes, Carpets, and Climbers 22" x 29" 2004

Hand-dyed silks, commercial cottons, synthetics, machine pieced, hand and machine quilted, hand embroidered.

I was born in New York City, raised in New Bedford, Massachusetts (a historic medium-size New England city surrounded on three sides by water), and have lived in Denver since 1974. I have a bachelor of arts degree in art history from Boston University. My formal education was a good background for the arts, but not as a studio artist. I was an artist without a medium. When I discovered fiber, I had found my medium at last.

Like many women of my generation and before, garment sewing gave me technical sewing skills. I learned from my mother at a very early age, and I am grateful to her for my intimate relationship with needle, thread and sewing machine.

For almost thirty years I have worked in the field of publishing: editing, writing, and graphic arts production. Since 1994, that has included editing for quilting publications, first as senior editor for *Quiltmaker* magazine and since 1999 as senior features editor for *Quilter's Newsletter Magazine*, the industry's first and most respected magazine, published continuously since 1969.

What first attracted me to making quilts in the late 1980s was the craft and technique. Almost immediately, I recognized the graphic design possibilities; the visual image

became more important than the quilt's function. Art quilts became my avenue to experimentation with fabric and using that play as self-expression. The planning or incubation stages of quiltmaking are engaging when the work is so full of potential and possibility. The active processes of stitching and handwork I find even more rewarding.

Being a person with an absolute worldview, I tend to interpret the world in black-and-white terms. My work often exhibits a fascination with opposites, contrasts, tensions: the products of nature as opposed to those from the hand of (wo)man, logic versus emotion, hard versus soft, transforming the organic into the geometric, unstructured/highly structured, light/dark, closed/open, content/technique, complementary colors, from our hearts or from our hands, defining things by what they are not.

Index I

Index III

Photo credits listed by artist, quilt name and photographer